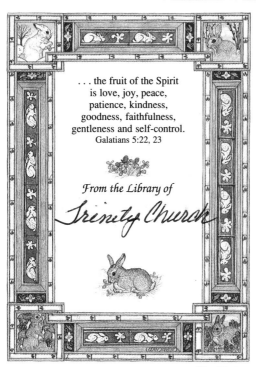

. . . the fruit of the Spirit
is love, joy, peace,
patience, kindness,
goodness, faithfulness,
gentleness and self-control.
Galatians 5:22, 23

From the Library of

Trinity Church

Caregiving

for your Loved Ones

Mary Vaughn Armstrong

Caregiving
for your
Loved
Ones

Mary Vaughn Armstrong

LIFEJOURNEY
BOOKS

David C. Cook Publishing Co.
Elgin, Illinois - Weston, Ontario

LifeJourney Books is an imprint of David C. Cook Publishing Co.
David C. Cook Publishing Co., Elgin, Illinois 60120
David C. Cook Publishing Co., Weston, Ontario

Cover illustration by Terry Julien
Cover and interior design by Ron Kadrmas
Production by Steve Johnson
Edited by Stan Campbell

CAREGIVING FOR YOUR LOVED ONES

Scripture quotations are from the *New American Standard Bible,* © the
Lockman Foundation 1960, 1962, 1963, 1968, 1971, 1972, 1973, 1975,
1977.

First Printing, 1990
Printed in the United States of America
95 94 93 92 91 90 5 4 3 2 1

Armstrong, Mary Vaughn
    Caregiving for your loved ones / Mary Vaughn Armstrong
        p.   cm.
    Includes index
    ISBN 1-55513-608-7
    1. Aged—Home care—United States. 2. Frail elderly—Care—
United States. 3. Caregivers—United States—Psychology. 4. Care-
givers—Services for—United States. 5. Adult children—United States—
Family relationships. I. Title
HV1461.A74 1990
362.82—dc20
                                                    90-6399
                                                      CIP

For Bob

Whose constant encouragement and
unswerving faith made it possible

"I am with you always, even to the end of the age"
(Matthew 28:20).

CONTENTS

Acknowledgments

I am forever grateful to our children: John and Rita, Matthew and Lori, Lee and Leslie, and Ann, who supported us without reservation throughout our caregiving season, and prayed this book into being.

I am also greatly indebted to many others, without whose help and advice this book would not have been written:

- Penny, though she would have wished it otherwise
- John Patrick Gillese, Canadian editor, author, mentor, and friend, whose vision was the beginning
- Linda Lawrence Hunt, writer, teacher, and celebrator of life
- Gail Fielding, innovative Whitworth College Library Public Services Supervisor
- The ever-encouraging North Spokane Writer's Critique Group
- Sue Travis, breakfast friend and patient listener
- Pastor Ted and Jane Hutchinson, whose letters and lives reflect the One they serve
- Dr. Joan G. Craig, M.D., for her wisdom, counsel, and common sense

- Howard K. Michaelsen, Attorney-at-Law, who kept me out of trouble
- Glenna Baxter Mills, B.S.N., for her expert help and suggestions
- The staff of Spokane's Family Home Care, who truly did
- Edith Shaw, friend and neighbor of the open door
- Azava Woods, whose help kept Penny in her home for two more years
- Kathy Bruner, whose enthusiastic and perceptive margin notes spurred me on
- Our extended family at Holy Trinity Church, especially:
  The Reverend Robert D. A. Creech, S.S.C.
  The Reverend Thomas J. Davidson, S.S.C.
  And finally the caregivers whose responses, prayers, and example formed the foundation of this book.

Mary Vaughn Armstrong
Spokane, Washington
August, 1989

Part I

Telling It Like It (Really) Is

This is a book for Christian caregivers—people who, by necessity or choice, faithfully care for an aging or disabled parent, spouse, or other relative. The loved one may live in the caregiver's home, a block away, or across town. Each day these caregivers turn themselves inside out in an endless marathon to meet their dependent relative's needs. They struggle with fatigue, overload, burnout, guilt, and much more.

They set up and clear away trays, endure stinging verbal abuse, ignore their own health, and stay home while friends take vacations. They see themselves in a mirror and wonder what hit them. They think thoughts they're ashamed of, and then, overwhelmed with remorse, weep in silence. A loved one's life rests in their hands, and it is an awkward burden.

Despite love, prayer, and the best of intentions, thousands of caregivers face defeat before they start. They are their own worst enemies, spending time, energy, and health as though they possess unlimited quantities of all three. They ignore caregiving's axiom: Protect yourself. *You* are your loved one's most vital asset.

Maybe you aren't a caregiver yet. But from the way things are going in your family, perhaps you soon could be. Barbara Eagan writes: "I recall the occasion when I first realized that my mother could no longer handle making a simple purchase on her own." Her mother, who has Alzheimer's and Parkinson's diseases, lives next door.

"We were in a store when the clerk asked her to come to another register, and she left her money on the first counter. This was a shock to me. I remember my anxiety and worry one evening when my father called us from the mall to tell us that Mother had not met him in their prearranged spot. I imagined her being robbed or mugged. We were quite relieved when we arrived at the mall and saw that he had found her. She had not understood where she was to meet him."

Perhaps your wife couldn't find her way out of the market the other day. Or maybe your dad's living room looks like a miniature Grand Canyon, with old magazines for the canyon walls. You realize something will have to be done. Soon. Oh, once in a while you pretend the problem doesn't exist, and there are some good days when things seem the way they used to be.

But something always goes wrong, like Mom's fall in the backyard last month. Thankfully, she wasn't hurt. But what about the next time? Or how about that call concerning the delinquent insurance premium when your husband hasn't forgotten a bill in thirty-five years of marriage?

Maybe the crisis hasn't hit yet, but it's on the way. And so you're reading this book, hoping for help. You won't find tips on how to brush up your nursing skills. You won't read how to give a bed bath or fix salt-free meals. This is a survival manual, meant to be read over and over. Caregiving is a major commitment, one of the biggest you'll ever make. The life of someone you love is at stake.

The book is divided into two parts. The first section identifies what *really* goes on in caregiving. The second describes the unlimited resources available to the Christian caregiver. Part one may be pretty scary, especially if you are contemplating bringing a disabled loved one into your home. Its three chapters take a no-punches-pulled look at caregiving's total impact on your life. It is designed to help you and your family realistically assess your caregiving readiness. The chapters will lead you into areas of emotional preparation that are far more important to giving care than sturdy equipment or balanced diet. The questions are blunt. Some will be difficult to answer.

Pray before you tackle this section. Ask the Holy Spirit to soften your heart and to slow you down for a while. Read it thoroughly; let it sink in. The three chapters you're about to study may not change your decision. But they will change your attitude, whether you're a caregiver now or soon may be.

Successful home caregiving is a lasting achievement. Many variables, including love, determine its outcome. But when it comes to caregiving, love alone is not enough. You wouldn't enter a tennis tournament without first learning the game. You wouldn't give a piano recital without years of study. Caregiving demands the same intensity of discipline and preparation.

It's no tea party you're considering, though your joys will be profound. So plan your new undertaking wisely and well. Take time to get acquainted with the job description. You'll be glad you did. So will your loved one.

[NOTE: Because three-fourths of those who give care are women, the pronoun "she" is used throughout the book when referring to caregivers. Also, specific friends and acquaintances will be quoted from time to time to give a broader perspective to the nature and experiences of caregiving.]

Chapter One
It Happened to Us

"**M**om, did you have a good flight?"

"I did once they got me to the right place."

Bob's eyes met mine over his mother's grey-blonde hair. "What did you say, Mom?" my husband asked.

"That plane let me off at the wrong city! They flew me back to Spokane, but then nobody was there to meet me."

The day before, the two of us and our college-age sons, John and Matt, had waited at the Spokane airport for forty minutes before Penny's plane landed. It was her annual Christmas visit from Phoenix, and we were eager to see her. What she was telling us twenty-four hours later didn't make sense.

Though she was in her mid-eighties, Penny had always managed well by herself. A hip transplant, needed because of her severe arthritis, allowed her to walk with the help of a cane. Daily medication controlled her congestive heart failure and circulatory problems. She adhered to a moderate life-style, protecting her treasured independence.

But that Christmas at our house was different from previous visits. A few days after the airport conversation, I watched her spend ten minutes trying to match a utility bill address with the envelope's see-through window. Finally, her hands shaking, she turned to Bob and asked, "Can you do this for me?"

A few days before Christmas, we all went out for a special dinner. In spite of the heated car, a wool afghan over her legs, and the shortest route to the restaurant, the next day Penny woke up with a wracking cough and stayed in bed.

From then on she slept much of the time and complained constantly of being cold. She looked thinner, and as I watched her I understood why: walking obviously hurt her. I suspected she'd lost weight because moving around her kitchen to cook was too painful.

On the morning she was to fly back to Phoenix, I walked down to her room around ten. Though her plane would leave in two hours, she was still in her bathrobe. As long as I'd known her, Penny was always ready to go before anyone else.

"I can't go," she told me, pointing to her closed suitcase on the bed. It was covered with small stacks of plastic-wrapped slippers, hosiery, Christmas cards, gifts, and stationery.

"Why not, Penny?" The night before she had seemed excited about going home.

"Because I can't open my suitcase. All those things are on top of it."

Time was short, so I smiled and made small talk as I helped her into a tailored navy dress and comfortable shoes. As Bob walked in the door I squeezed her robe into the suitcase. In Phoenix, good friends met her plane and drove her home. They had already filled her refrigerator with food and turned on the heat.

She was back where she wanted to be, but we knew she needed help—fast. That night we called Azava, a faithful friend who had helped Penny in many ways through the years. After some discussion, the three of us worked out a long-distance caregiving arrangement. Azava would prepare three hot meals a week and deliver them to Penny. Each would be large enough for at least two servings.

Azava agreed to make sure no old food remained in the refrigerator. She would also do light housekeeping chores, shop for Penny, see that she paid her bills on time, and make sure she took her medications. In return, we agreed to send a check to Azava each month for her time and work. Kirk, the neighbors' son, would continue to mow the lawn. Another close friend would telephone and stop by regularly.

This system proved highly successful and made it possible for Penny to remain in her home for two more years. But as time went on, she needed more and more help. Often she refused to answer the doorbell or phone. Once she fell in the kitchen and couldn't get up. Fortunately we phoned her, unaware she had fallen, and when she answered we learned she was sitting on the floor. We alerted Kirk's mother, Carol, who cut the back screen to get in and then helped Penny to her feet. We had stretched the time in her home to the limit, and then some. Our long-distance caregiving was in its twilight.

Not long after her fall, we could tell during one of our weekly phone calls that something ominous had happened. Penny's normally expressive voice was a monotone. She initiated no conversation and spoke only when asked a direct question. Early the next morning we called her doctor and arranged for him to examine her in his office.

Azava told us later that on the day of the appointment, she helped Penny bathe and dress. Then she backed the car out, warmed it up, and walked with Penny to the edge of the porch. But Penny would go no farther, and nothing Azava said made any difference. After an hour of coaxing, she helped Penny back to the living room.

The next day the doctor went to see Penny at her house. He visited with her, examined her, and watched her walk using the cane. Later he told us gently, "I'm afraid your mother can't live by herself any longer. She can barely walk, and is quite confused. She's losing urine, but what worries me most is she doesn't care. She has always been so meticulous about herself."

The doctor explained that Penny had an advancing senile dementia, caused by many small strokes in her brain. Called multi-infarcts, they probably began years before. She would steadily grow more forgetful and confused.

We had always planned to care for Penny in our home, if and when the time came. One reason was because Bob, who was an only child, had years before promised his Danish-German mother she would never go to a nursing home. We have since discovered that many adult children with elderly parents feel the same way.

Glenn and Carolyn Bradley care for his widower father, who has Alzheimer's disease. "None of us in the family felt good about putting Dad in a nursing home while he can be handled here at home," reported Glenn. "We feel we can offer a quality of life not possible in nursing homes."

David and Mary Lou Sprowle, who provided home care for his mother, echoed the same feelings. "I always thought that family should be cared for by family," said Mary Lou. "Nursing homes seemed the same as a direct death sentence. I openly condemned those who sent loved ones to 'old storage.' I still do not like nursing homes, but now I understand the need for them."

"I felt my mother would be happier in my home than in a nursing home," wrote Liz Cox, who cared three and a half years for her mother. "Also, it would be easier on me than going over to see her every day."

"I felt responsible to give Genevieve all the care I could," wrote Ted Dexter about his wife of over fifty years. "I realize that she is God's creation and that I am one of His creation. As a member of 'His body,' I feel responsible for the care of my wife."

In addition to my husband's long-ago promise and the fact that we were Penny's only living family, we wanted her in our home for other reasons. For one thing, home care was affordable. A good nursing home costs $18,000 to $22,000 a year—far more in some areas. At that rate, Penny would be impoverished in a short time. Researchers at Harvard Law School found that nursing home costs could bankrupt 46 percent of single 75-year-old seniors in just 13 weeks.

We had heard about small, licensed group homes that care for three to five patients and are much less costly. Many of the owners, frequently those who have already raised their own families, lavish tenderness on their patients in a renaissance of care.

Nevertheless, we wanted Penny with us for as long as possible. Later, in talking to other caregivers, we learned we weren't alone in our preference for home care. Fewer than six percent of America's elderly (up to age 85) are in nursing homes. Of those over 85, only one quarter require institutionalization. All others are either cared for by family members, with varying levels of assistance, or remain in their own homes. The latter option would have been far too expensive for Penny, who would soon need full-time help.

Another factor in our decision to choose home care was the fifth commandment: "Honor your father and your mother, that your days may be prolonged in the land which the Lord your God gives you" (Exodus 20:12). Of course, parents can be equally honored in a care facility, and we were fully aware Penny might one day need one. Had I worked outside our home, we would probably have chosen another option. But since we were in a position to offer home care, we were glad to do so.

Despite her confusion, Penny trusted us and was eager to live in our house. Before her illness, she probably would have fought to keep her independence. But now her bewilderment seemed to cushion the sadness of giving up her own home. Within the givens of her condition, we knew she would be happiest near her family. And by providing the best care we could, we hoped to work through some of our own grieving for her eventual death.

Home care also gave us opportunity to repay, in a small way, the quality of love and care she had lavished on Bob as he grew up. Later it would be good to know beyond a doubt that we had done everything we could. Meanwhile we could enjoy Penny every day. She might be limited in certain ways, but she could take part as fully as possible in her own family's daily life.

We also liked the model of family solidarity that home care gave to our four children: Ann, John, Leslie, and Matthew. As we talked to them about our plans for their grandmother, they enthusiastically supported us. They may not be faced with the same set of problems as Bob and I age, but they would have hands-on experience in coping with crisis.

By faith, we sensed that God was providing us a rare opportunity for spiritual growth through caregiving. "Consider it all joy, my brethren, when you encounter various trials, knowing that the testing of your faith produces endurance. And let endurance have its perfect result, that you may be perfect and complete, lacking in nothing" (James 1:2-4). But at that time we were unaware how much endurance we were going to need.

The absence of Penny's close friends was a strong disadvantage of moving her to Spokane. In Phoenix, many of them had died and others were in poor health, but she knew no one in our city.

Another drawback was our family's lack of elderly caregiving experience. Bob and I had kept my 83-year-old grandmother in our home while she was recovering from a stroke, but she died a month later. My mother died at 58, after a bitter two-month battle with intestinal cancer. Both Bob's father and mine had died shortly after a heart attack.

Yet we had a lot of things going for us (close family, Christian commitment, love, and desire), and my nursing background proved invaluable as we threw ourselves into high gear to get ready. I phoned agencies for information, arranged for transfer of Penny's records from her doctor to ours, and set up the room where she would sleep.

She was to stay across the hall from our bedroom in a room that had been used often for guests. We rolled up the hooked rug and installed in its place a warm beige carpet. We also added a large picture wall heater, the kind hotels use because of their safety. Months later I realized that most of our preparation had been physical—cozy rugs, warm heaters, a bed with side rails, an adjustable wheelchair, a geriatric recliner, and so on. I had no idea that the most difficult part of caregiving would not be what I *did* for Penny, as demanding as that was. The hardest part of all would be emotional—dealing with what I *felt*.

The chapters that follow will explore the not-very-pretty thoughts Bob and I had as caregiving dragged on—thoughts confirmed by dozens of other people who provide home care. We were ashamed to admit what we were really feeling. When almost everyone tells you what a wonderful thing you're doing, it's embarrassing to express your innermost thoughts to them. But little by little, we learned how. First we learned to be honest with each other, and then with God. He patiently taught us His way to handle our feelings, and that's why this book was written.

After two months of preparation, we were as ready as we would ever be. Because of Penny's condition and the distance between Phoenix and Spokane, we decided to fly. We bought two plane tickets to Phoenix, and made return reservations for three. At that point, neither Bob nor I had much idea of what was ahead. We simply wanted Penny with us for as long as we could manage it.

That positive thought sustained me until we walked into her Phoenix bedroom many hours later. The room was dimly lit, with dark mahogany furniture and overgrown bushes covering the paned windows. Penny looked up at us from her chair and smiled, much too politely. I realized she had no idea who we were.

Azava had dressed her to greet us, in blue patent leather heels and a pin on the collar of a blue dress Penny had sewed for herself years before. A hairpin dangled from the austere bun that replaced her once softly waved hair.

Hours later we inched her from the wheelchair to her bed. We lifted her legs onto the bottom sheet and covered her up, watching her trembling hands pick at the covers. It seemed impossible this was the same beautifully groomed woman who smiled at me each day from our hall's photograph gallery. Long years as a nurse helped me reassure her. But on the inside, I was trembling, too. Right then I wanted to be anywhere but here, doing anything but this.

Our caregiving season crept up on us slowly, the way late autumn blends into winter, giving us time to prepare. Sometimes a loved one's catastrophic illness or accident forces caregiving to begin within hours. But however it starts, assuming total responsibility for a parent's or spouse's life is formidable.

Ted Hutchinson and his wife Jane take care of his mother in their north Seattle home. Ted's mother is a victim of osteoporosis and mild senile dementia. She had fallen, fracturing the bone below one knee, and could no longer walk. "I felt scared that it would ruin our lives by draining away family time," Ted wrote, "yet I was relieved that Gramma was now in our care, in a much safer environment."

Other caregivers feel helpless, apprehensive, scared, angry, eager to be an example to children and friends, or relieved not to have to maintain two houses any longer. Some feel overwhelmed. Renée Kuehl wrote, "Care began following my father's suicide. He had been Mom's caregiver, so Mother then needed emotional support, too."

Glenn and Carolyn Bradley's caregiving literally began overnight. His mother, who provided all care for Glenn's father with Alzheimer's disease, had a sudden, fatal heart attack. Glenn and Carolyn felt "scared, shackled, noble, worried, tired, loving, and very thankful we had made earlier decisions (retirement, building a house) so we were in a position to take on the new challenge." Carolyn remembers feeling "overburdened . . . but we wanted to do it and could do it as a team, at least for a while."

The first night Bob and I were in Phoenix, listening to Penny's slow, deep breathing, we spent a long time in prayer. We were convinced God had called us to care for her. But back in Spokane the task had seemed far more manageable than it did here, twenty feet from her room. My own ambivalence surprised me. I genuinely wanted to take care of her. But a twenty-four-hour-a-day commitment, not knowing how long it would last or what lay ahead, was frightening.

We spent four more days in the home where Bob grew up. I found the dented, heart-shaped aluminum mold that Penny used to make red Jell-O on Valentine Day. I cleaned the dusty, hand-cranked cheese grater her mother had brought from Denmark.

When Azava arrived each morning I followed her around, memorizing Penny's routine as the reality of her helplessness sank in. By the end of the second day I had bought diapers, decided showering was too dangerous, and substituted bed baths. Through Penny's doctor, I arranged for a Phoenix public health nurse to make a home visit. Her practical suggestions, such as adult rubber pants for the long trip ahead, helped and reassured me.

The day the three of us were to return to Washington State, Bob and I were up at five. After breakfast I knocked on Penny's door and walked in. Nothing could have prepared me for what I found.

Penny sat on the edge of the bed, her lifeless hair in thin strands around her shoulders, molding a bowel movement with both hands. I yelled for Bob, somehow keeping my voice steady. Together we cleaned her up, and after the world's fastest manicure, got her dressed while Azava cleared out the chest of drawers and filled the suitcases. Then the three of us helped Penny into the car. Bob went back to take apart the Port-a-Potty and wrap it in cardboard. I anchored the edges with my legs, hoping my nylons wouldn't run, while he secured the awkward package with a rope. My stockings held up, and fifteen minutes later we were ready.

Penny sat expressionless in the car, gripping her purse as we loaded the walker, Port-a-Potty, and suitcases. We raced through the house for a final check, then closed the door for the last time.

Six months later, Bob and Leslie would return to pack the rest of Penny's things and list the house with a realtor. Until then, Penny's wonderful neighbors and a routine patrol would guard its contents. As we drove away, Penny's home for half a century disappeared in the distance. Her face appeared a puttied mask, but my heart told me she knew. I squeezed her hand and prayed for strength.

Penny was hoisted onto the plane strapped firmly to the seat of a narrow, metal aisle chair. The steward knelt on the floor and rotated each of her feet in tiny circles until she could sit down. She stared straight ahead the entire flight, hands spread over her leather purse. But when lunch was served, she picked up her fork and ate every bite. That was a prophetic key to the future, but we didn't know it then.

Despite sunny weather and good food, it was a very long flight. Bob sat beside his mother; I was across the aisle. From time to time I looked down at the clouds below as I prayed. Five hours later, on April 9, 1986, we landed in Spokane. Our son John met us, his car heater on high to protect Penny from the spring wind.

At our home an hour later I helped Penny into her prewarmed bed. She was too worn out to eat. Not long afterward, Bob and I tiptoed down the hall and fell into our own bed, exhausted. I woke up several times during the night, listening. If Penny needed anything, she had nobody but us. The responsibility I felt was crushing. Our season of caregiving had begun.

> "Lord, I feel as if my own life is inside a helium balloon, and the string just slipped out of my hands."
>
> *"I love you, My child . . . and I have a tight hold."*
>
> "Even in this, Lord?"
>
> *"Even in this."*

Chapter Two
Will Love Be Enough?

*"*F*or where you go, I will go, and where you lodge, I will lodge. Your people shall be my people, and your God, my God. Where you die, I will die, and there will I be buried. Thus may the Lord do to me, and worse, if anything but death parts you and me."*

With these inspiring verses from the Book of Ruth taped over our kitchen sink, Bob and I slogged through the first weeks of caring for Penny. We drew up medication schedules, planned range-of-motion exercises, baked cookies, and tried each day to think of something special for her.

Except for meals, she preferred spending most of the day in her room. I felt like a jeans-clad young mother with an infant pack on my back. But instead of a baby, it held my mother-in-law. Whatever I did and wherever I went, Penny hung on my mind twenty-four hours a day. Was she warm? Did she have enough to do? Was she missing Phoenix too much? Were we spending adequate time with her? Almost all caregivers, I later learned, share these feelings.

"Our family life went down the tubes," wrote Mary Lou Sprowle, whose mother-in-law couldn't walk and had congestive heart failure and lung problems. "My husband, daughter, and myself never went anywhere as a unit . . . one of us always had to stay with Grandma. Our yearly vacation was out. We went on a weekend trip for our birthdays, leaving our daughter at home . . . her gift to us. Grandma was with us at all times—if not in body, in spirit."

For Bob and me, Sunday mornings were the worst. We team taught a Sunday school class, and loved it. We always left the house at eight-thirty, giving ourselves time to set up our classroom before the nine o'clock service.

I needed an hour to dress, but Penny required a minimum of two more. Not counting our own breakfast (we quickly discovered bagels and cream cheese to eat on the way), we needed three hours before we backed our car out of the garage. In other words, caregiving meant we got up at 5:30 A. M. on Sunday—earlier if we wanted *toasted* bagels.

We orchestrated those three hours with the precision of an Olympic event. I'd get up, make the bed, shower, and put on everything except my church clothes. Then I'd slip into an old robe and dash to Penny's room, where I'd give her a bed bath, get her into the wheelchair (a five-minute process), and push her up to the tea cart. I would set the wheelchair brake and join Bob in the kitchen, where we would scramble eggs, butter toast, pour juice, and hurry it back to Penny's room.

While she ate (if she didn't need me to remind her), I'd change into my church clothes. Then I would return to Penny, coax her to finish, and help her into bed again. During this time Bob toasted the bagels and started the wash.

By the time we arrived at church, we had done half a day's work. We both felt and definitely looked it. The words from Ruth, "Where you die, I will die, and there will I be buried," were a mocking echo in my tired brain. I sat in church wondering who would go first: Penny or I. In less than a month, the verses from Ruth were dog-eared and bedraggled. So was my attitude.

What went wrong? We had planned carefully, set up a routine, rented proper equipment, and tried to do it all right. But there were two things we had neglected to plan for: Bob and me. Our lives were vanishing in the distance, strapped to a flatcar named fatigue. Did we love Penny? Unquestionably. But caregiving, we were discovering, goes far beyond love. Love was a given—an immovable mountain around which everything else flowed. Yet loving Penny did not make her care easier—only bearable.

Would the rest of our lives be like this? Had our desire to provide the highest quality care been only a fleeting saccharine rush of childish idealism? What if the day arrived when she couldn't be left alone at all? Would Bob and I ever eat breakfast together again? Was home care really the best choice for Penny? Where did we fit in? Had we made the biggest mistake of our lives?

Like thousands of other caregivers, our approach to the task was utopian and inadequate. We had brought our newborn babies home one by one, and within weeks couldn't remember life without them. We had been confident that Penny's arrival would be the same. It wasn't. A new baby is small and light, filled with hope, responsive, and, most of the time, sweet.

But dependent adults are exactly that: dependent. They are on the downward side of physical ability. Instead of learning to walk, they may be forgetting how. Instead of being easy to pack along to the grocery store, they often require heavy, awkward equipment. They get short of breath and become embarrassed, discouraged, and cross.

After one visit to the doctor, it was obvious that Penny's outings would be limited to the front and backyards. It took Bob and me ten minutes to pry her out of the car's front seat into a wheelchair. From that time on, I shopped alone. But I always rushed, uneasy about how she was doing at home. It wasn't long before I realized that medication, equipment, and home-cooked meals were only a tip of the caregiving iceberg. It was time to take a hard look below the surface.

"Offspring who are concerned about their dependent parents' health and happiness usually think of taking them into their home," said Don Bogart, who with his wife Donajeanne cared for his blind mother for thirteen years. "Some people may be capable and able to handle it. Yet because of the burden involved and effect on your own mental and physical health, I do not ever recommend doing this, as hard as it may seem to say so."

Donajeanne urges, "Don't do it unless absolutely necessary. Familiarity does often breed contempt. The loving has to be worth the bad times or it can be disastrous to everyone! You have to remember it is also hard on the recipient of care and on innocent bystanders. I'm glad we did it, but I wouldn't advise it. A person really has to search his or her own heart and *pray, pray, pray!*"

As Bob and I discovered, a momentary flash of bigheartedness pales overnight against caregiving's realities. Perhaps, as you read this book, you are already involved in caregiving. Or maybe you see the need coming: Mom, Dad, or perhaps your spouse simply isn't doing very well. Your loved one is managing, but you sense it can't last.

You've thought about taking care of them yourself, in your home. But you're not sure whether you *can* do it, or if you *should*. You want to make the right decision and have it continue as long as possible. You couldn't bear to move your relative somewhere else in two months. Your heart tells you to go for it, but your mind holds back. You want to know more about what you're letting yourself in for.

Whatever your situation, a hard look at the following pre-caregiving inventory will help. Because every family is unique, no single question is the most, or least, important. What may be a major caregiving stumbling block to you may be a mere pebble to your neighbor. As we explore the hidden parts of the home care iceberg, the only prerequisite is honesty with yourself and with your family.

1. Have you visited any small group homes in your area? Any convalescent or continuing-care retirement communities? Have you talked

to other caregivers? Read anything about caregiving? An abundance of excellent material is available. A number of resources are listed in the appendix in the back of this book. Start there and then plan a trip to the library. Gather as much essential background information as you can. You may never use the facilities you visit or the suggestions you read and hear. But everything you discover about the viewpoints of other caregivers will help.

2. If you're to be the primary caregiver, how is your own health? Have you struggled with severe depression? Perhaps even thought of suicide? Is it wise to subject yourself, and the relative you love, to this added stress? Do you have physical limitations that could interfere with your loved one's needs? What happens if caregiving makes your bad back go out again? Or pushes your blood pressure into the danger zone? If something happens, do you have an alternate plan, or does Mom begin to pack?

3. Is every person living in your household willing to help care for your relative? If even one person opposes it, you're looking at a flashing red light that spells caution. Taking care of someone in the home taxes every family member. Nobody under the same roof should be allowed to file an exemption.

4. Do you and/or your husband work outside the home? If so, how will your loved one manage while you're gone? Can he or she remember when to take medications? Will he wander outside and forget the way home? Might he even forget that he has a home? And how about you? When you return from work now, do you have much energy left? If you become a caregiver, you'll have less, not more.

29

5. With God's grace, are you prepared to live your own life around the edges of your caregiving ministry for several (perhaps many) years? Much will be suggested about how to do this in Part II, but the truth needs to be told up front: If anybody's life gets put on hold, it will be the caregiver's.

6. How's your family communication? Do you openly share feelings and problems? Are you a chin-up, be-perky-or-die family? Do you bury emotions in a subterranean level until they erupt in a mile-high geyser? Are door slamming and tire peeling high on your family's list of coping techniques? If you answered yes or supplied creative additions to these questions, watch out. Caregiving will make a poor situation worse, not better.

7. Two parallel bars support successful caregiving: adequate help and time away. Much more will be said about this later. For now, one question: Are you willing to grip those bars and admit you're not superwoman?

8. How little sleep is enough? What happens if caregiving cuts into it? If your relative wanders through the house at night, who gets up to find her? If she needs oxygen and pulls the tube out, who replaces it? If he's in pain, who gets the medicine for him? You can cut down on sleep for a while, but if the situation becomes permanent you'll have nothing left. You may end up needing oxygen yourself.

9. Do you have any prior nursing experience? Did your mother care for someone in the home while you were growing up? Can you draw on that role model? A woman who is a caregiver for her husband shares, "During my teen years

my mother cared for her grandfather, her aunt, and her mother in our home until their deaths. I did some of the 'legwork' for the latter two, but only now realize what her burden was."

10. How big is your energy tank? Who else in your life draws from it? Toddlers? Teenagers? Husband? Job? Can you keep going when you're down to almost empty, or might you run out of gas when things get rough? Can you manage Christmas decorations, cookies for the choir, wrapping two dozen gifts, and Grandpa's range-of-motion exercises? Be honest. The life you save may be your own.

11. If you should manage to get away from caregiving for a few hours, are you ready for company? Your loved one will go right along with you, like Harvey the invisible rabbit. "Jane is just like a new mother with her first baby-sitter," said Ted. "After about an hour away— often when we're just beginning to relax—Jane starts worrying about Mom." Caregiving has a long, long leash.

12. Do you and your family have a temperament conducive to caregiving? When a loved one's hearing gets fuzzy and memories dwindle, your simple comments and suggestions may need repeating three or four times. When you hear "What?" for the fifth time, it's easy to lose your cool.

13. Can you approach caregiving like an observant meteorologist? Seasons begin and seasons end. But some winters make you wonder. Your loved one's death at home may gracefully conclude your caregiving season. But what if his winter should go on and on? If your burden grows unbearable, can you face taking an hon-

31

est, unbiased look at home-care alternatives? Convalescent and nursing homes are only one option. Again, explore the appendix for resources you could one day need.

14. Have you realized that your loved one might sometimes be deeply discouraged or depressed, and you won't know why? Some days he or she will be troubled, sad, tearful, or silent, and you can discover nothing about the cause. When that happens you can't walk across the parking lot, unlock your car, and drive away. Your loved one's mood may go on for days. That kind of lingering discouragement muddies the emotional water of any home.

15. How does the physical structure of your home relate to your loved one's abilities? Will Grandma see the thirty-foot drop off the balcony? And if she does, will she back away or strap on her parachute? Does your front window command a scenic view of a freeway, when Grandpa lived all his life in the country? And how about the bathroom? Can you bear bolting handgrips into the imported tile you waited twenty years to buy? Can other rooms be locked for privacy when desired?

16. Is caregiving a necessity for you, or simply a preference? Either way, it's important to be honest. Take careful inventory: exactly why do you want, or perhaps not want, home care for your loved one? Even if you have no other alternative, identifying your motivation will help. Every caregiver feels differently:

   • "I wanted to be near my husband (who had Alzheimer's disease), to be there whenever he missed me, to be sure his every need and wish was attended to."

32

- "I personally said that the patient could not come into our home. I knew she would require 24-hour care, and 'good old me' would be elected. There was room at my sister-in-law's and money to hire care."

- "My mother, who gave me care with love when I was helpless as a baby, deserved love with care from me when she was helpless (as a very old woman). It seems to me nothing can compensate for care from those you love, if that care is sufficient to keep them relatively well and pain-free."

- "There wasn't any other choice. I felt it was my duty, I guess."

17. Have you considered household pets? If cats are an integral part of your home, what about Grandpa's cat hair allergy that used to set him sneezing when he turned down your street? Does Grandma's arthritic Lhasa apso move in with her (the one who never caught on about housebreaking)? Don Bogart emphasizes, "The hardest part of twelve years of caregiving was putting up with her stupid dog."

18. How are the medical facilities in your area? Can you put together a workable arrangement? Is your doctor also Grandma's? Have you discussed home care point by point with that doctor? Is he or she willing to work with you to help it succeed? Is a hospital reasonably close by, in case of emergency? Is a surgical supply house in your area where you can get needed equipment? Do they pick up and deliver?

19. How do you handle rejection? When you give 110 percent of yourself and your good inten-

tions are thrown back in your face—sometimes literally—how will you respond? Much caregiving involves assisting someone who is irritable, suspicious, belligerent, ungrateful, and who doesn't have a clue who you are. If that person happens to be your parent or spouse, rejection can cut like a knife.

20. Like a juggler, can you keep more than one ball in the air at a time? Caregiving will strain every relationship in your life to some degree. Can you balance one person's special needs and everyone else's? Or will your family secretly wonder, "What about us?"

21. Is your caregiving commitment tough enough to withstand disapproval from family and friends? How about the times when you are on the ragged edge of fatigue and someone all rested and radiant tells you how to do a better job? Can you bite your tongue, or will caregiving turn your family and friendships into World War III?

22. What are your *real* feelings about the person living, or about to live, with you? Your bottom-line feelings matter a great deal. If a two-hour dinner with your relative used to require three hours of prayer, don't expect things to change because she can no longer dress herself. Weak relationships plus the demands of caregiving add up to stress with a capital "S."

Possibly your season of caregiving crept up slowly, like a few ants at a picnic. So far you're managing, handling the problems one by one. Or maybe it took over your life in the space of hours, like food poisoning. One morning you felt fine. By noon you were flat on your back. However your caregiving begins, it's never easy. Your loved one needs help, and you offer it. For a while your devotion clothes the task in a short-lived glow. But sooner or later reality hits, and with it guilt by the carload.

This is my husband, the caregiving wife thinks, *and he needs me! But what about my own life?*

"This boy loves everyone he meets," marvels the mother of a severely disabled child. "Why can't my own love measure up to his?"

Mom did so much for me, the adult son chides himself. *How can I grumble because now she needs help?*

All caregivers entertain similar thoughts. They may even express them aloud, if family communication is good. Such symptoms indicate a common illness: caregiver jet lag. Her mind says her loved one needs help. But her heart and body haven't yet gotten the message.

It's a lot like flying from the United States to Europe or Australia. Your mind and watch tell you it's ten in the morning when you land. But your body doesn't catch on as quickly. It aches, yawns, and forgets things. You long to go somewhere quiet, pull the covers over your head, and tune out the world. But you can't. You're in a new country now, where cars honk, cafés perk coffee, and bright sunlight splashes across the children's playground. It's morning. And you're exhausted.

Many of us have felt that kind of jet lag. It produces a short agony, usually cured by one or two good nights' sleep. But caregiver jet lag won't be routed so easily. There is no quick fix. With or without sleep the guilt lingers, accompanied by a host of feelings as foreign as a rare parasite. On top of everything else, memories of the caregiver's used-to-be life refuse containment:

- "We used to go to the symphony on Friday nights, but he can't climb the stairs anymore."

- "She's embarrassed to eat in public, so we stopped going out."

- "Bowling was a big part of our family's life, and Mom loved it. But getting her in and out of the car, then into a wheelchair—it's too much."

- "Mom and I spent part of every summer at the cabin she and Dad built. But when I take her there now, she cries. So we don't go. I really miss those times."

- "Mom, my beautiful mother who used to sing all day long, just shuffled her deck of cards for the thirty-eighth time today."

The caregiver's used-to-be feelings rise to the memory's surface like vegetables in a simmering soup. The heart looks back and remembers, while the mind interlocks with the present. *That was then and this is now* . . . the caregiver will pace between the two realities for months, searching for accommodation. In due season, it will come. The sparkling used-to-be times won't forever disappear. They will be boxed up and stored away with ribbons of memory. At a later date, when it's safer, they will be tenderly reopened.

The urgent, this-is-now times will grow and multiply, revealing a beauty all their own. When the season of caregiving is over, they, too, will be placed in boxes. And as unbelievable as it may seem, many caregiving memories will someday become treasured used-to-be's.

"I'm scared, Lord. I feel as if I'm at the edge of a giant forest, and the trees are so tall and strange. I've never come this way before . . . ."

"Take My hand, little one, and don't let go. I know the way."

"Even in this, Lord?"

"Even in this."

Chapter Three
Counting the Cost

"**M**y mother-in-law was 93, dirty, and slowing down. Her home was almost unlivable. After our son married, we moved her into our home so we could do our best for a wonderful person that we loved and respected. She would be warm, clean, and cared for until she died. Very simple, or so we dreamed."

Maybe you feel just like Mary Lou Sprowle. You love your failing relative. You want to do the right thing for everyone, but it's all getting more and more confusing. One day you feel like arranging your loved one, all cozy and warm, right in the middle of your family. The next morning a friend asks you to bring two dozen cookies to vacation Bible school and you burst into tears.

Deep inside, you're afraid of this caregiving business. You sense it might require a 180-degree turn on your life, and you're less than thrilled. Things won't get better or return to normal, you're realizing. They'll get more difficult.

In the last chapter we took a hard look at what happens to you and your family when you bring a dependent person into your home. We now need to look at some of care-giving's concealed price tags, the ones that don't show up at first glance. Caregiving is expensive in ways that have nothing to do with money. If you decide to go ahead with it, you'll stand a far better chance of success if you examine its hidden costs now.

Cost #1: Loss of Freedom

Most people list loss of freedom as the most expensive part of caregiving. Because there are so many additional things to do, there is far less time for everything else. A simple trip to the grocery store becomes a nerve-racking task if Mom is likely to set fire to a tea towel or decide to visit the neighbors—wearing only her curlers. An over-night getaway may be impossible. Vacations could become a memory.

"Our first priority was always their care and needs," shared a long-distance caregiver of both parents. "Every-thing else had to come second."

"It is important for the caregiver to realize that once entered, the job becomes a total commitment of time, effort, and love, which sometimes may be strained," wrote another caregiver who with his wife cared for both his parents. His father had diabetes and later a severe stroke. His mother was legally blind.

Laverne Kerns shared the care of his wife, a victim of Parkinson's disease, with his son and daughter-in-law. Though thankful he could provide care during her last illness, Laverne freely admits that "it abolished all free-dom." His son Steve confirmed that feeling: "The last year and a half of her life, all of our schedules revolved around caring for Mom."

Carolyn Bradley observed, "The hardest part for us was the lack of spontaneous freedom to go skiing, horse-back riding, or other things together or with our children."

"I have no freedom," wrote Geneva Canada, a retired teacher whose husband had two strokes. "The bedroom and kitchen are my world. Also the bathroom, if I hurry."

Cost #2: Chronic Fatigue

Fatigue comes in many packages. There's the good, tired feeling after cleaning up the flower beds in spring. There's the bottomed-out feeling after a week with the flu. Then there's the kind of fatigue my mother used to refer to as being "bone tired."

The caregiver is almost always bone tired. A good night's sleep (if she can get it) will recharge her battery only for another twenty-four hours. Much of her life gets put on hold. Unanswered letters pile up. And should she find an hour when she could answer them, she'll use it to sleep.

"One of my biggest problems is that I do not have enough time to do everything that needs to be done," wrote the caregiver whose retired husband had a stroke, leaving one side of his body paralyzed. "I have problems making up my mind. My husband used to cast the deciding vote, but his opinion is now not always reliable. I still succumb to anger and depression. I am constantly tired."

"The hardest part of caregiving," said Geneva, "was fatigue both in body and soul."

Even when a loved one is oriented and able to care for himself, fatigue shadows the caregiver. Suppose you're single and you've had a day at the office that would tax the angel Gabriel himself. Before caregiving, you would come home, put on friendly old clothes, take the dog for a fast walk, perhaps treat yourself to an ordered-in pizza, and open a new book.

But with someone else at home, everything changes—no matter how dearly you love him or her. When you get home you must talk, whether you feel like it or not. After all, poor Mom's been cooped up in the house by herself all day long. You're so saturated with people you'd enjoy a week on a deserted island, but you know you should talk to her.

One of the reasons she's living with you is because she couldn't manage very well on her own. So you can't leave her to fix her own dinner. Anyway, that's not very sociable.

You would order in the pizza—and she'd probably love it—but the spices upset her stomach and she's not supposed to have salt. So much for that. By the time you fix creamed tuna and Jell-O for dinner, engage in some conversation, and try to act interested, you're too tired to read anything. You go to bed and hope tomorrow will be different.

"Fatigue was my worst enemy," wrote Donna Ring, who provided across-town care during her mother-in-law's last illness. "I was there all day. I changed her and bathed her and did her laundry. The hospital lost her bridge, so I cooked chicken and vegetables and pureed them in the blender. With her being in her own home and me in mine, it was simply a matter of time before my house fell apart."

Physical fatigue comes from many sources, including the double or triple work load that goes with caregiving. There's at least twice as much washing, cooking, and cleaning. If your relative is incontinent, there will be additional laundry: towels, washcloths, sheets, clothes, and nighties. Between cooking and washing, you must continue to be a nurse, pharmacist, occupational and physical therapist, and friend.

Cost #3: Isolation

As the demands of caregiving grow, the leash shrinks. Where two years ago a couple could slip away for an hour or so, the day may come when they're afraid to leave. Or if one goes, the other stays home to be sure Dad doesn't fall out of bed or decide to repair the dishwasher dial.

Isolation gradually tightens its grip. Your loved one asks to stay home, fearing the exhaustion, embarrassment, and stares from going to public places. Reluctantly, you agree. Your participation in the garden club, Bible study group, or even simple visiting continues to decline.

Missing once isn't bad. Twice isn't bad. But hundreds of absences from things you value take a toll. Your excursions become kitchen to bedroom to family room to laundry room and back to kitchen.

Isolation is particularly painful if the caregiver is single or taking care of a spouse. Unless she fights ingeniously to maintain her own life, a single caregiver may find herself a recluse: "Mom's got a little cold . . . . Maybe I'll not bother with choir practice tonight." And for the caregiving spouse, going anywhere without the beloved is achingly difficult. It flies in the face of a lifetime of shared experiences.

"I feel like a rat in a cage," shared Mary Lou Sprowle, "that functions when a bell rings, always on time, doing the same chores."

"There were no vacations or outings for us during the last year and a half," remembers Steve Kerns.

"Our social life was very restricted," wrote another caregiver. "I could not leave him alone for a minute. I even took him with me to the store. We went to dinner a time or two, but it was hardly worth the struggle. We had no vacation until the second year, and then just overnight. He did not want people to see him 'the way he was.' "

"The hardest part," wrote a wife whose husband has Alzheimer's disease, "is the marital imbalance—assuming all the responsibility, and loss of a *partner*."

"Until the last six months I had taken Genevieve to a number of restaurants," reported Ted Dexter. "But I do not take her anymore, because her eating habits make it difficult."

"Glenn's mother suffered most from loneliness—not being able to talk to her husband about their children, their memories, or anything," remembers Carolyn Bradley. "She also felt isolated, as friends came less frequently and she got away less. Her isolation was partly due to not letting people know how confined she was and not asking for help."

Cost #4: Role Reversal

Sometimes dependent loved ones retain control of their mental faculties. They know who the caregiver is, and they express gratitude. "Mom suffered with such dignity," wrote Renée, Kuehl who with her husband Jack cared for her mother at home for three years. "She never complained, rarely criticized, and was always grateful."

But more frequently, physical illnesses alter and decrease brain function. The parent whose clothes you proudly wore to play grown-up now undresses herself on the sidewalk. The parent becomes the child. The child, regardless of age, becomes the parent: coaxing, wheedling, encouraging, scolding. All caregivers find this reversal of lifelong roles extremely uncomfortable.

I had always been daughter-in-law and hostess to Penny, eager to please her. Before she'd visit I would plan special meals and outings. When she arrived I would consult her for ideas about projects and plans. Then overnight, I became both daughter-in-law and caregiver. The somersaults of the role reversal left me dizzy.

"The most difficulty came when they couldn't remember what I had told them only a short time ago," recalled the person who cared for both parents at once. "They became childlike, but I couldn't treat them like children or talk to them that way."

"It was hard to adjust to the change of character I saw," wrote Steve. "I lost Mom before she physically died."

Cost #5: Permanent Change in Household Routines

When somebody needs ongoing assistance, he or she probably requires special equipment, schedules, and procedures. Caregivers rarely examine this costly price tag. One morning they suddenly realize that everything in their house is different, and they panic. An honest assessment now may reduce shock later.

All that equipment must go somewhere. Medicines must be safely stored away. Somebody must administer them each day. Mom's or Dad's special diet and favorite foods must be available. Grandma may be in the way when your grounded teenager stages a heated try for the family car. Or she may wander into private rooms, startling, frightening, or embarrassing family members inside.

Loss of space and privacy accompany caregiving. Jane described a continual feeling of having "a shadow." She never knew when her mother-in-law would come into the room unannounced.

"Giving up the privacy of my home," wrote Donajeanne Bogart, "was the hardest part of caregiving. Many times I felt our home belonged more to Mom than to us."

Reality is harsh: once caregiving begins, former household routines and relationships won't return to the way they were. Period. Everything changes—some for the good, some for the not-so-good. When caregiving ends, things will go back to how they were. Not before. Routines and procedures can be streamlined only so much. The hospital bed, lift, wheelchair, walker, commode, recliner, and other necessary equipment are there to stay. Grandma lives there now, and that reality impacts every part of the household.

Cost #6: Disapproval

This hidden price tag always comes as a jolt. Your heart is large and loving, or you wouldn't even consider caregiving. You think and pray about it, roll up your sleeves, and plunge in. But sooner or later you get criticized, often by family and close friends.

"We received criticism from other family members because we were caring for Mom," remembers Steve Kerns.

"Why do you want to kill yourself?" a friend asked another caregiver.

Mary Lou Sprowle wrote, "My mother-in-law has congestive heart failure, lung problems, and doesn't get around. She is in a wheelchair all the time." Her husband David added, "She went to the nursing home for twenty-four hour care. Relatives are upset now. Some think we did the unpardonable by putting her in a home. Others agree with us. Great family turmoil came from our decision."

Disapproval usually springs from the soil of concern for the caregiver, but not always. Whatever its origin, it hurts.

Cost #7: Guilt

Guilt is the caregiver's uniform, with her wherever she goes. If she leaves her loved one, she feels guilty. If she stays with him and wishes she were somewhere else, she feels guilty. No matter what she does, her heart tells her it is not enough.

Mary Lou wrote, "All the while I hated myself. I knew all I did was in vain, and that God hated me for the way I felt. I knew I was a failure."

Cost #8: Sexuality

Does caregiving, for the married couple, mean celibacy? Quite possibly. At best, it means a greatly diminished physical relationship between husband and wife. Judge for yourself, based on this sampling of comments:

- "After my blind mother-in-law had been in our home a good many years, I became resentful. Our relationship certainly suffered."

- "My frequently tearful emotional state affected our marriage relationship. The old laughter (what I call 'the joy factor') was missing."

- "We worked together pretty much, but there were times I resented the patient and how she was affecting our lives. It got to be that the first thought when we wanted to do something was, *How will this affect Mom?*"

- "We were always tired. We were always under stress. We complained to each other. We became stronger. We retreated to 'Camp David' (a sign I made and hung over our bedroom door). If the situation got too bad, we just went in there and hoped it would all go away."

- "The hardest part was balancing my attention between husband and mother. It did cause conflict. My husband seemed to resent not being able to do anything without making a lot of plans."

- "It drives a wedge that affects communication
  and feelings. Fatigue and exhaustion took their
  toll on our sexual relationship. I had the desire
  to 'just be held,' but pulled away from the one I
  love most because of the expectation of sexual
  demand. I just couldn't face it."

But even though a physical relationship may diminish,
caregiving can at the same time build a deep and
altogether different bond between partners:

- "I think our relationship is stronger as we accept
  this challenge as a team and recognize new
  strengths and love in each other. Our own
  closeness is only affected when we fall short of
  sleep, and so far that isn't often."

- "It brought out a whole new dimension of loving and caring. It's a pretty special wife who is
  willing to share her home and life with a father-
  in-law who requires constant watching and
  help day and night. I love her more than ever
  for the way she makes him welcome and still
  continues to support me."

- "As I saw my husband tenderly, compassionate-
  ly, and lovingly care for my mom, our marriage
  became richer. He was great and I never took
  that for granted."

- "To think my husband cared as he did, both for
  me and for my mother, is rather overwhelming.
  He did not verbalize his emotions, but his
  actions spoke not only of his love for me but
  also of his love for our Lord. This definitely
  strengthened our relationship and blessed my
  life as well as others."

Yet even as the love between a caregiving husband and
wife deepens, its physical expression is not likely to return
to normal until the rest of their lives do. Husband and
wife in dual caregiving roles have only so much emotional

and physical energy. When it's used up on Grandpop, it's gone. Bed becomes a haven for one thing—survival.

Cost #9: Lack of Time

Insufficient time is like water flowing through a groove on the surface of a rock. The caregiver's day is the water. Her life is the rock. She rushes through weeks, months, and years, scrambling to make up lost time. She feels constantly pressured, and she pushes herself beyond all wisdom.

"There is no time to write letters, pay bills, dust the furniture, cook interesting meals, go shopping, or keep appointments," wrote one caregiver.

"The hardest part of caregiving," remembers Renée, "was finding *time*. Dividing time between the two homes became a challenge of time management."

Somehow caregivers learn to function with permanent stress. But this leads to unpleasant and sometimes ominous side effects. We'll talk about this in chapter eleven.

Cost #10: Unspoken Fears

As one season blends into another, the caregiver grieves the approaching loss of her loved one. But there is a flip side to her feelings: she grieves also for herself. Adult children mourn two losses: the treasured parent or spouse, and their own childhood and youth. Caring for Mom, Dad, or a spouse in the home magnifies both bereavements.

This may be the first time in their lives that adult children come to grips with a singular reality: if Mom and Dad don't live forever, I won't either. The fact is obvious, yet most of us avoid this issue. And though few caregivers admit it, many shadowbox with another unspoken dread: If Mom or Dad got this disease, will I get it, too? These fears can be profoundly disturbing.

Cost #11: Caregiver's Health

Because their loved one's needs are more immediate, many caregivers defer their own. One devoted wife cared for years for her helpless husband, ignoring her recurrent rectal bleeding. When she finally sought help, surgery revealed intestinal cancer beyond treatment. She knew better than to neglect her own symptoms, but like legions of others, she put her relative's needs above her own.

Cost #12: Emotional and Physical Abuse

Most caregivers will have to deal with the issue of abuse—even people who buy sweaters for their dog and give Christmas cookies to the paper boy.

A few months after Penny arrived, her toenails needed cutting. Her toes were almost impossible to separate, twisted from the tight, pointed-toe shoes of the 1920's. Her toenails were thick and hard.

First I took care of her bed bath, rolling her from side to side, rubbing her back, combing and braiding her long hair, applying lipstick and cheek color, and trying to make conversation. Then I set to work on her toenails. It was a bright Saturday morning, and I longed to be gardening, running with the dog, or enjoying a cup of coffee in the warm summer sun. So I rushed—and accidentally cut one toenail too close to the quick. Penny flinched, jerked her foot away, and cried "Ouch!"

At that point I got frightened because I didn't care. I was sorry I'd hurt her, but a side of me felt she deserved it. I wanted to be outside, not working in her hot room while she lay there like the dowager queen.

I wrapped a small bandage around her toe and carefully finished the job. As I worked, I came to grips with the fact that I'd hurt Penny and didn't feel one bit sorry. Me, an abuser? Almost. I knew I needed help. Right away. It wasn't long until we arranged for homemakers to give Penny her bed bath and personal care several times a week. I looked forward to those days like a child on Christmas Eve.

In spite of all my good intentions, nursing skills, knowledge, and commitment to Penny, I had sailed eerily close to abusing her. The toe healed up in two days, but my memory didn't. That experience showed me the tissue paper curtain that separates caregiving and abuse.

Could it happen to you? You bet. One million elderly persons are abused each year by their own children. When the caregiver's needs collide with the patient's, anything can happen. Sick, dependent people are exasperating. They can be passive, impossible to satisfy, complaining, and oblivious to all needs but their own. Those kinds of behavior can trigger anger and frustration in an already exhausted caregiver.

Not all abuse is as obvious as a bleeding toenail—intentional or not. Emotional abuse can be subtle and deadly, such as ignoring the patient's questions or personal milestones, refusing to listen, or isolating a loved one.

We've all read horror stories of physical abuse. We turn away from vivid pictures detailing atrocities such as abandonment, infliction of pain, confinement, and worse. *Not me,* we think! *Not to my mom, dad, or spouse!* Probably not; hopefully not. Nobody plans to abuse a loved one, yet statistics prove the problem is a tragic national phenomenon.

Take a hard look at the patient and yourself. If you get tired enough and your loved one disagreeable enough, is there a potential for abuse? This caregiving price tag is very costly, and there are no returns.

Cost #13: Back-Burner Anxiety

Caregiving is riddled with recurring emergencies in many forms: some small, others not so small. Often two or three happen at once. Perhaps your loved one chokes on her toast and turns blue while you dial the paramedics with shaking hands. Or maybe your relative's emergencies are less life-threatening, such as skin breakdown, refusal to eat, or constipation.

"Just before Christmas," wrote Mary Lou, "my husband's mother had a 'spell' one evening. She didn't know us and went out of control. We called the life squad, and she was in the hospital over Christmas."

The caregiver lives in a perpetual state of watchfulness, assessing her loved one's condition as they talk. The result is a back-burner anxiety, the expectation that, sooner or later, something will go wrong. And she's the one on twenty-four hour duty.

Cost #14: Heartbreak

Caregiving is precisely what the word suggests: giving care. But there comes a time when nothing more can be done. Despite family support, medicine, laughter, exercises and megadoses of love, the beloved relative goes downhill. To those left at the top of the slope, this is the most painful part of all.

"I do find it difficult not to feel depressed as I watch my mother slip away, little by little," shared Barbara. "It is rare to get one complete sentence out of her per day. She is down to 115 pounds. Alzheimer's and Parkinson's are the largest problems. The loss of her dignity and quality of life—the personality of the mother who loved and cared for me all of my life—is the hardest."

Diane Price remembers that, "The emotions involved in not being able to communicate as mother-daughter were difficult."

Another caregiver recalls that, "Watching someone slowly die for seven years drains everything."

Dayne Nix, whose wife had a brain tumor, spoke for many when he shared that, "Seeing the patient's condition gradually deteriorate was the hardest part."

Edith Shaw, a registered nurse who administered kidney dialysis at home for her diabetic husband, said that the hardest part "was the frustration of not being able to restore him to a healthy human being."

"Seeing my mother become a child and not know anyone for the last two years of her life," remembers Kaye Kepple, "was like a death . . . a loss."

"The hardest part," wrote Laverne Kerns, "was accepting the fact that the effects of Parkinson's were too much for me, the M.D., and the specialist."

Another caregiver's mother had multiple small strokes at the same time her father learned he had advancing prostate cancer. She shared that the most difficult part "was watching my beautiful, wonderful parents deteriorate before my eyes, and being helpless to alter the course, though we had turned every medical stone possible."

A point is reached where there is nothing more to adjust, nothing more to fix. The heartbreak of caregiving is one of its steepest costs.

Your desire is to honor your father, mother, spouse, or other relative. If it weren't, you would not be reading this book. But honoring is a matter of spirit, not geography. The most important thing right now is the appraisal of what you are contemplating.

You may decide, for many reasons, that you must say no to home caregiving. From there you'll move into a new kind of honoring—bringing food, flowers, games, and bushels of love into the place you select for your loved one.

"When they are in the nursing home," wrote David Sprowle, "your most important job continues. Do not forget them! Visit often . . . once or twice a week is good. We went every day for a while, and she was not adjusting. When we spaced out our visits, her attitude got much better. They just need to know you are there." Honoring doesn't stop simply because your loved one lives somewhere else.

Perhaps you have examined the caregiving price tags one by one. Maybe you retraced your steps and picked up several tags for a second or third look. You turned them over and over in your mind and heart. You wrestled with the reality, with all the areas that invade a caregiver's life. You talked, prayed, cried, and searched your soul. One part of you resists involvement in this draining assignment. Yet everything else longs to get started.

You have opted for home caregiving. You've studied its price tags. You realize its cost. And you want to go ahead, at least for a while. If so, let me walk with you into the areas that will appear as surely as winter rains, for there is much joy—and satisfaction beyond words—in what you are about to do. The path will be strewn with difficulties. The cost, as you now know, will be terribly high. So also, beloved caregiver, will be the rewards.

"Father, I just want to take care of Dad the way he always took care of me. But I feel so weak . . . ."

"My daughter, it is I who will become your strength."

"Even in this, Lord?"

"Even in this."

Part II

You—The Other Half of the Equation

Reading through Part One probably wasn't easy. You worked through a series of hard questions and grappled with the costs of being a dependent person's lifeline. The fact you're still reading means you're seriously considering, for better or worse, caring for your loved one at home. You may want to give it a try for as long as it seems right for you, your family, and your relative.

Maybe you really don't have any choice, but you desperately need to know more about it. Perhaps you *do* have a choice, and in your heart of hearts sense that God is calling you to provide home care. You realize He isn't insisting that you sign up for ten-plus years. But you're convinced He is asking you to try.

We're going to move ahead now, into the nuts and bolts of caregiving from *your* perspective. If you need to know how to give Mom a shampoo in bed or where to buy adult diapers, look in the back of the book. You'll find lots of suggestions. And don't worry—a whole chapter is devoted to the problem of finding help.

But we're going to focus on *you*, not the one you're caring for. Loving the patient begins and ends with the caregiver. If you go under, so does your relative. In the chapters ahead, you'll learn how to cope as you give care day after day after day. You'll be encouraged to get a little tough and be a little selfish. You'll learn how to take care of yourself—how to survive.

We'll look at aspects of caregiving that, sooner or later, you're going to encounter. We'll identify problems and discover specific strategies to deal with them. Caregiving requires an enormous emotional investment. As we've seen, it isn't about rocking chairs and chicken soup. It's far more serious, far more complicated.

But there is wonderful news for those committed to Jesus Christ, those trusting Him to lead the way. They possess coping methods most of the world never dreamed of. He gives us resources that don't cost a thing, aren't difficult, and don't require a Ph.D. to understand. They are refreshingly simple, as was every message from the Lord Jesus.

He never calls us to a new endeavor without first equipping us for it. He gives us a complete starter pack when we set out, and the refueling we need along the way. Right now, as you read, He is in the process of providing every tool you'll require in your caregiving journey. So smile a little, hitch up your backpack, and let's go.

Chapter Four
Three to Get Ready

"It has been about six years since I recognized the first symptoms," wrote Ted Dexter. His wife Genevieve, mentioned earlier, suffers from Alzheimer's and Parkinson's diseases, repeated bladder infections, an enlarged heart, and incontinence. The two of them recently observed their fiftieth wedding anniversary.

"One day Genevieve told me she didn't believe she would drive the car anymore. Not long afterward, during income tax time, she kept putting me off about collecting the data and so forth (which she had always done). She had also paid the bills as they came and taken care of the bankbook. I had to take over those responsibilities. The housework was noticeably neglected. Other signs of a problem were physical: When she had a bowel movement on the toilet and was not able to clean herself properly, I found it necessary to take over this aspect of sanitation. Gradually she has lost interest in carrying on a conversation. At the present time, she speaks only three or four words a week."

Ted's caregiving season took six years to unfold. Others materialize in less than a day. "Glenn's mother was caring for Daddy," reported Carolyn Bradley, "when she suddenly had a heart attack and died. We want to give him more personal, loving care. But we didn't expect it to be so total, so soon."

In Part One, we looked at what really goes on in caregiving. We examined the gap between expectations and reality. We learned that, like getting married or having a baby, much of caregiving is learned through practice and experience. You wouldn't say "I do" without reading and preparing. You wouldn't bring an infant home without buying diapers and lotion. Caregiving is no different; it's just the other end of life.

Maybe you have a large family, but because of distance or a thousand other reasons, you're the one unanimously elected to coordinate what happens next to your relative. Or maybe you're already a caregiver, simply because there is nobody else. So should you skip this chapter on preparation? Not at all. You can't prepare for everything, but you can do a lot.

Preparation is caregiving's framework. Whether you have five months, weeks, days, or minutes, preplanning for the season beginning in your loved one's life will reap rich dividends for both of you—even if you're already a caregiver.

Tracking down medical supply houses and emergency facilities may score zero on your interest scale. Searching out (much less, joining) a caregiver support group may be your idea of wasting time. Being put on hold by overworked switchboard operators may send you up the wall. If so, you're in good company. Most caregivers feel the same way. But all agree their preliminary research paid off handsomely in confidence and knowledge. Best of all, they felt less isolated.

Do you remember the childhood rhyme: "One for the money, two for the show, three to get ready, and four to go"? When it comes to caregiving, "three to get ready" isn't just a catchy phrase. As the poem says, getting ready divides itself into three categories: your loved one, your family, and you.

Preparing Your Loved One

When caregiving begins, too often the person who needs help gets ignored or forgotten in the scramble of decisions. Maybe your loved one is crystal clear mentally, but can't live alone because of a physical problem. Or perhaps he can fast-walk with the best of them, but thinks it's 1945 and he just got out of the Army. Whatever your relative's condition, here are some suggestions to help you prepare for his or her caregiving.

Pray

Begin by prayerfully acknowledging your own feelings. Whether you're caring for a spouse, parent, child, or other relative, you're feeling all sorts of thing: grief, loss, fear, inadequacy, guilt, and lots more. And, truth told, you'd probably like to run away from the whole thing. In prayer, pour out all your feelings to your heavenly Father. Allow yourself time to weep, mourn, and be silent before Him.

Pray, too, about what's happening to your loved one. Be specific about his symptoms, limitations, and fears. Tell the Lord about your own failures: how you wish you were more patient, how scared you are, how much you'd like to be doing something else, how tired you already feel. And take comfort that those feelings are caregiving's work clothes. Everyone wears them.

As you pray, you'll find yourself accepting more of your situation. It may not get easier, but it will get clearer. Prayer slows you down, deepens your understanding, and broadens your perspective.

Think

When we moved Penny out of her home, she couldn't walk to the bathroom, cook her meals, or write a check. We had no doubt about what we needed to do. But it's often not that clear-cut. A person's health does not usually collapse all at once. Maybe arthritis prevents grocery shopping, but Mom still loves to cook. Maybe she forgets to turn off the sprinklers, but never the grandchildren's birthdays.

If your health began to deteriorate, what would *you* want? Two-thirds of all widows live alone. Almost none of them want to live with their adult children. They, as we, treasure their independence. With this in mind, explore the "what ifs." What if we arranged part-time help for Mom in her home? What about meals-on-wheels? What if someone helped with her heavy housekeeping? What if she had a ride to an adult day-care center? What if a nurse's aide or visiting nurse stopped by once or twice a week? Could some of these options keep Mom on course a while longer?

If your parents live in the same place, is Dad able to help with Mom's care? Does he want to? Does he need help, too? Can he drive? *Should* he drive? Can he write checks and manage financial resources? If you answered yes to most of these questions, probably the best way to help Mom right now is to give Dad a hand. Almost everyone is healthier and happier in their own home, even when they need some help to stay there.

Elderly people worry most about two things: loss of health and loss of money. As time goes by, they are often (but not always!) relieved to discuss financial matters with one or more of their children. Without preempting the parents' control, an adult child can listen, gather information, offer advice (if asked), and reassure them.

These early stages of caregiving can often be handled from a distance: across town, across state, or even across several states. For a while, a Saturday afternoon visit to Mom's may be enough to clean her house or apartment and bring in groceries. She'll love the company and enjoy getting out to shop or have her hair done.

But sooner or later, that Saturday afternoon expands into a full day. You may need to start giving Mom a call every twenty-four hours or oftener, to be certain she took her pills. Then one day the whole thing demands too much of your time, becomes too cumbersome, and just isn't safe. At that point, something has to give.

Talk

When it comes to any sort of change, your loved one deserves the courtesy of a well-thought-out, caring talk. Wouldn't you want the same thing? Even if a relative is way beyond meals-on-wheels or part-time help, including him in decisions about his future is part of honoring him.

Pray long about this talk before it takes place. Watch for opportunities: perhaps an article about aging or the illness of one of your relative's close friends will provide an opening. Plan on one or two hours, and allow for more. Lead into the topic gently. Don't jabber about moving Dad in with somebody the day he mistakes the living room couch for the toilet bowl. He's already feeling bad enough.

Tell your loved one how much you love him or her. Speak as you would like someone to speak to you, not as though you're talking to a toddler who deals in one-syllable words. Honestly describe what you see happening: "Mom, we're concerned. Since Dad died, we know how hard it's been for you. We really worry about your being alone so much now, and about your safety. We've had some ideas. Can I tell you a few?"

Explain gradually. Keep the conversation positive. Hold your loved one's hand if it seems natural. Laugh. Be patient. Remember that your suggestions will probably come as a horrible shock to your relative. Soften everything with kindness, even if you've said it all a dozen times before. No matter what words you use, it is devastating for anyone to be told they aren't capable of caring for themselves any longer. You'll need a wheelbarrow full of patience.

Talk about specific options where your loved one might safely live. Discuss retirement complexes, low-rent church facilities, shared housing, licensed and carefully screened group homes, and other alternatives that provide assistance in a flexible environment. Last of all, ask the most ignored question in caregiving: "Mom, where would *you* like to live?"

Mom will undoubtedly announce she'll stay right where she is, thank you. Most people, as they grow older, detest change. You'll need to circle back to this question again and again. Your relative may cry and try desperately to change the subject. Be loving, but be firm, no matter how torn up you feel inside. Repeat the problems you see.

Then, somewhere along the line, give The Invitation: "Mom, Bill and I have lots of space—in our home and in our hearts. Would you consider moving in with us? We know there would be lots of adjustments. But we're a family, and we believe it could work out wonderfully. What do you think, Mom?"

This is the question Mom would probably rather die than have to deal with, so it's terribly important how you say it the first time. You may even want to rehearse. Try to sound as convincing as you possibly can. She'll murmur all kinds of things about how "I never wanted to be a burden." Strongly reassure her. Respond gently to every objection she raises. Soften the whole idea by suggesting, "Why don't we try it for a while?" This buys you some time and helps preserve your relative's self-direction.

Talk about how you'll help her move and how she can bring furniture, pictures, and anything else to her room(s) at your home. Discuss meals with her, and cooking, and shared chores—even if you have to exaggerate. Talk about things Mom or Dad could do during the day, especially if you'll be gone. Stress how much better the family will feel, knowing she's safe.

This scenario is, of course, the ideal one. Sometimes, despite everything you do, your loved one can't or won't cooperate. This makes your task heartbreakingly difficult. It may well require intervention by a person both you and your relative have confidence in: a minister, priest, friend, or counselor. But even when the going gets rough for both of you, keep talking and reassuring. Obnoxious behavior may be a reaction caused by fear and embarrassment.

Let your loved one know you wouldn't be making these suggestions if you didn't think he needed help. Pat his shoulder or hug him often—even if you're not used to it. Let him know you're with him in all this, that together you're going to work it out. And through it all, keep in mind that the way a season of caregiving begins has a lot to do with the way it ends.

Often, adult children make promises to elderly parents which later become impossible to carry out. If you made a promise you know you can't keep, talk it over with your loved one. Point out how circumstances have changed. You'll feel guilty because you promised Mom she could stay in her house always. At the time, you meant it. But during the past year she's slipped in the tub four times, won't open any doors, and forgets to eat. Loving her now means moving her where she will be safe. You don't want to do it and you'll still feel guilty. But you have no choice.

Preparing Your Family

Sometimes, as with Bob and me, there is no other family to help with caregiving decisions. In that case, buckle your seat belt—you're it! But if you have other relatives who might give you a hand, the second stage of preparation involves every one of them.

Sooner or later, somebody in a family discovers that things aren't going at all well for Mom, Dad, or someone else. That person (probably you) becomes responsible for alerting other family members. The name of the game, when it comes to family participation in caregiving, is communication. Your goal is to get everyone involved in one way or another. Whether you discover trouble with your loved one during an annual visit, or whether you live next door and see him every day, you need to let the others know. Your family can't help if they aren't aware of what's going on.

Their responses will be as varied as their personalities. One catches the next plane to Dad's city. Another snaps, "So what am I supposed to do? I live two thousand miles away." Yet if family members fail to respond appropriately, it is usually because nobody has taken the time to tell them, in graphic detail, what's really happening. They're simply expected to figure it out. If they don't, they're labeled detached or uncaring.

Be creative with your communication. Not everyone can afford to hop on a plane. And in the preparation stage of caregiving, that response won't help a whole lot anyway. You can, of course, pick up the phone and arrange a conference call, allowing give-and-take between family members in several locations. Or you could write a letter detailing Mom's or Dad's problems as well as possible solutions. Make a copy for every relative and tell them you need to hear back by a certain date.

Also consider using a cassette tape. Reams of information can be poured onto tape, mailed off, and answered in the same way. Videotape is another possibility. Perhaps you could film an interview with Mom and/or Dad on a rented camcorder. Each family member could view it, then mail it to the next person on the list. Remember that old adage about a picture being worth a thousand words?

Before you phone, write, or tape, make a written list of things you want to cover. Try to use concrete examples of what your loved one is or isn't doing that worry you. This should help the others feel the same concern you do.

Remember to give everyone time to react to what you are telling them. Be prepared for lots of questions, perhaps angry words, or even out-and-out denial: "Mom just needs a good rest!" Some family members may cover up grief and shock with excessive busyness. They may rush to their parent's home and wear everyone out, including you, with a wild binge of cooking, sorting, and cleaning.

Be patient. All such responses are variations of grief. Everyone expresses deep sadness in a different way—even in your family. It can be agonizing to realize that Mom, Dad, or another relative can't take care of themselves anymore. Give your family some time and space to react.

After they know what's happening and have had some time to let the truth sink in, explain that you need input from each of them—in person or by letter, phone, or tape.

Suggest a date for their replies. This is also the best time to propose a family conference when all of you can get together to make plans. Have them tell you when and where they could be available to meet.

After you hear from everyone (or all you think will reply), pick a date and location for the conference and let them know. If at all possible, this meeting should take place before any kind of caregiving begins. Call or write the family members who didn't respond. Give them a chance to help, even in a small way. If they refuse (and this happens surprisingly often) there is little you can do. Occasionally, another family member or trusted third party can mediate the situation.

You can't force anyone to help, but for your loved one's sake, you must move ahead with your planning. You'll feel hurt and angry when people refuse to get involved. After all, you need every bit of help you can get. Confess those feelings to God, and then let them go. Don't waste precious energy on a situation you can't change. Above all, weed out any seeds of bitterness that could take root in your spirit's soil.

Once the family conference date is set, you'll begin another vital area of caregiving: gathering information. Your family can prepare as a unit, dividing up the areas to be investigated. Match talents of family members to preparation needs. Stretch out or combine assignments, depending on numbers of people involved. Below are the major areas you'll need to know about.

Medical

Perhaps a family member with an interest in science could meet or talk by phone with your loved one's doctor. You may also want to consider evaluation of your relative by a specialist in geriatrics (treatment of the aged). If you are moving your relative many miles, ask his or her doctor to suggest a new physician in your area. Or perhaps your own doctor would agree to care for your loved one. When this is arranged to your satisfaction, ask the former doctor to transfer all records to the new one.

After your loved one has been examined, obtain a diagnosis, some idea of overall health, and what to expect as time goes on. Ask the physician to review each and every medication your loved one is taking. Bring all bottles of medicine with you for the doctor to see, including vitamins, prescription medications, and non-prescription drugs. Ask about dosages and possible side effects. Discuss your relative's mental state, possibilities of improvement, and what you might do to keep him or her as healthy as possible.

Would the doctor work with you in home care? For how long? What would he or she suggest if your loved one's needs exceed what you can offer at home? What would happen if you couldn't continue as a caregiver? Would the doctor make home visits if your relative were unable to get to the office? Would he accept Medicare assignment (what Medicare pays) as his fee? How often would the doctor want to examine your relative? Are your views and the doctor's compatible regarding care at the end of life?

Community Resources

Someone needs to explore all the possible options for caregiving in your relative's city or town. Keep in mind your loved one's wishes. See what's available in the community along the lines the two of you discussed. Look into the cost and eligibility requirements of the housing possibilities listed earlier.

Find out the charges for skilled and unskilled nursing care, and how this is usually billed. Ask if each organization is licensed by the state and participates in Medicare and/or Medicaid. A few phone calls will provide much information, whether or not you intend to use it. Most places are happy to mail brochures, cost breakdowns, and other details.

Finances

A family member with a gift for numbers might look into this essential area. Proceed carefully and get all the details. You need to find out exactly what your loved one owns. If a house is involved, you need to know if there is a mortgage. Can the house be sold and the proceeds invested to help your relative? Could it be rented out? Does it need repairs?

Does your loved one have a union pension, such as civil service, carpenter's, veteran's, teacher's, or other? Any nontaxable holdings? A money market account? Certificate of deposit? An annuity? Social Security? An IRA or Keogh account? Life insurance? Investment dividends? Find out what checking and savings accounts he or she holds, and the balance in each. There could be several accounts in more than one bank. Don't forget to look over your relative's most recent state and federal income tax returns to determine yearly income.

Maybe your loved one has been living in a one-room apartment on a Social Security pension. Or maybe he has spent a lifetime preparing for his later years, and has more than enough to meet his needs. Whatever his status, during your investigation you'll feel as if you're snooping into his most private matters. It's hard. In fact, it's awful. But it must be done. Remember: the foundation of helping your loved one is knowing what's available to work with. Again, you have no choice.

A word of caution: Money issues can split families deeper and faster than an earthquake. Get the facts. Be prepared to present them at your family conference in as detached a manner as possible.

Health Insurance

The person who talks to your loved one's doctor will probably be elected to look into his or her medical insurance. Whether retired or not, if your relative is 65 years or older and has enough credits for work under Social Security, he or she is eligible for Medicare. This federally administered health insurance program is divided into two parts. The first, Part A, is hospital insurance. Part B is medical insurance for physician's and surgeon's charges in and out of the hospital.

People who aren't Medicare eligible will have to pay a monthly premium for their Part A and B coverage. Though

Medicare pays eighty percent of many health needs, including equipment and medication, it does not cover most home care, custodial nursing home care, or care in a residential facility. Many other coverage gaps remain, so check with any local Social Security office for specifics of Medicare benefits and pamphlets explaining coverage. You may also want to inquire about the Supplemental Security Income (SSI), which provides monthly benefits to low-income people who are elderly, blind, or disabled.

You should also look into what forms of supplemental health insurance your loved one may have. Keep in mind that 37 million Americans have none at all. Medicare supplements, called Medigap, cover many services and expenses Medicare does not. Medigap insurance, purchased as individual policies or group plans, can be obtained through commercial insurance companies, Blue Cross, Blue Shield, or health maintenance organizations (HMOs).

Be sure to personally review the fine print in your loved one's medical insurance program. Find out exactly what is and is not covered—hearing aids, drugs, dental care, glasses, and so forth. Get professional help with this if possible. Call your own insurance agent or check with your state insurance commissioner's office for assistance. Some older persons are overinsured, and may be paying additional premiums for duplicate coverage.

Your relative may qualify for Medicaid, the state-federal health program which helps pay most medical bills for low-income people or those who have exhausted their own resources. If your loved one may be eligible, contact your county assistance office. Neither Medicare nor Medigap supplemental policies cover long-term illnesses or conditions requiring nonskilled custodial care. Only Medicaid provides unlimited custodial care in a nursing home—to those who qualify.

Though most older persons believe they have nursing home coverage, few actually do unless they are Medicaid eligible. However, many insurance companies now sell long-term care coverage, and also riders which can be added to an existing policy. The premiums and pay-outs vary, but this coverage offers skilled, intermediate, and custodial care in a nursing home, as well as home health services. In addition, some employers are making affordable, long-term care insurance available to employees and their spouses, parents, and parents-in-law.

Commercial, long-term care policies for nursing homes vary widely in cost, depending on the age of the insured, group vs. private rate, and benefits purchased. Annual private policy premiums could go to $2,500, and people over 79 may not be eligible. Policy provisions and exclusions vary widely from state to state, and should be thoroughly checked.

Nursing homes cost anywhere from $20,000 to $60,000 a year. Because most people must meet these costs themselves, two out of three persons in nursing homes become Medicaid eligible within a year. Even three home-health aid visits a week may cost up to $10,000 annually.

"I am responsible for investing and trying to make my parents' money stretch," wrote one caregiver. "I feel panic at times to be able to cover everything."

Assess the financial portion of your preparation thoroughly. How much money is available for your loved one? What sort of health insurance, if any, does he have? Will more money be needed? Check the appendix of this book for resources concerning Medicare, Medicaid, and other insurance information. Then brace yourself for the family conference and be prepared for a barrage of questions.

Attorney

Perhaps someone in your family has an understanding of the law and could set up a meeting with your relative's attorney. If your loved one doesn't have a lawyer, you can ask friends for a referral or check the white pages of the phone book for "Community Service Numbers." You'll probably find a listing for legal assistance with several numbers. Also check "Lawyer Referral Service" and "State Bar Association" for your state. Last, look in the yellow pages under "attorneys."

New health legislation passes in every state each year. One or two hours' legal consultation will save you much grief later. The time for that is now, before things get out of hand. When you set up your appointment, ask the attorney how much it will cost and what you should bring along.

When you meet, ask him or her about your loved one's will, if you haven't yet located it. If there is none and your relative is mentally sound, find out how to set one up, if at all possible. If your loved one isn't competent, what can you do now to prevent future problems?

You may want to consider a possible legal guardianship, joint ownership, or conservatorship. Be sure to ask about the possibility of obtaining a power-of-attorney. This retains your relative's assets in his name, but allows you or another designated adult to manage them. A durable power-of-attorney also allows your relative to specify treatments and health care he may or may not want. Needless to say, this requires written permission from your loved one.

Also ask about "Interspousal Transfer of Assets," available in some states. Generally speaking, this means that fifty percent of a couple's combined income from Social Security and pensions would be used for the relative in poor health. Medicaid would take care of the balance, leaving the couple's other assets untouched. For people with spouses or other dependents, this is vitally important.

The Family Conference

When your family all gets together, approach the meeting with three goals in mind: (1) to discuss facts, (2) to express feelings, and (3) to make decisions. Ask someone to pray, then spend a few minutes in silence before the loving God who is guiding each one of you. If it seems appropriate, by all means include your loved one in this conference.

Allow time to verbalize grief, anger, and sadness. One person can keep things on track so chunks of time are not wasted. Make up your mind that this conference won't end until you're agreed on the next step for your loved one.

Now is when everyone's detective work pays off. Let each family member share what he or she has learned. The health expert would be a good place to start, sharing everything from his talk with the doctor. Move on to what's available in the community that might meet your relative's needs. Then take a sobering look at the financial realities. Last of all, spice it up with what the attorney said.

By the time all this is reported, it's probably time for a break. Laugh. Let the information overload ease up a little. Then get back together with the sole purpose of coming up with a course of action. The plan you make today may not be forever, but determine to wind up this conference with some sort of strategy defined. Spend several hours matching your loved one's needs with the available options, and decide what is best.

Perhaps you're the caregiver already, or soon will be. It's right about now in the family conference that, one by one, heads turn to you. The whole family thinks you're wonderful—a little crazy, perhaps, but wonderful. And now's the time for you to get tough. Oh, keep smiling at them. But don't forget that while the strategy defined during the remainder of your conference will help your loved one, it will also directly affect *your* life.

You may not know it, but you now have a title: You're a primary caregiver. That means you've got the whole ball of wax. You're it. Mom's going to live with you, if she doesn't already. Or maybe it's your spouse, and all the children have come home to see how you're doing and how they can help. Okay, here's your chance. Tell them!

Now that you have that fancy title of primary caregiver, it's essential that somebody agree to be a secondary caregiver. Who will that person be in your family? Who takes care of Dad when you leave for a week or two? Watch the faces of your family when you bring this up—they'll all grow pale. Repeat the question. You are going to insist on some sort of vacation every six months or so, and regular time off each week—more often if you can swing it. Who takes over then?

What if this year's flu virus puts you in bed for a week? Or you slip carrying out the trash and break your ankle?

What happens then? Is there money to bring in round-the-clock nurses? If not, what will your family do? This is an imperative issue if you're single or a caregiving spouse.

"I feel that a family of brothers and sisters could work together as a unit," wrote Mary Lou Sprowle. "They should be able to keep a parent at home . . . in all of the children's homes, or in one home with everyone helping. My husband and I were alone, and we felt the pressure. Never try to do it alone. There *must* be support. The caregiver *must* get away for as much time as it takes to keep family life as normal as possible."

"Attention and planning must be given in the event of illness, an accident, or the death of the caregiver," urges Glenna Baxter Mills, B.S.N., Home Health Care Management Consultant for Mills, Pollin, and Associates, Inc., in Walnut Creek, California. "My mother-in-law worried a great deal about what would happen to Grandpa if she should die, realizing that it would mean institutionalization for him. During the early period of his illness (Alzheimer's disease), before others were aware of the situation, they were alone in their mountain home. Grandpa fell on her, fracturing her leg in four places. It took thirty minutes or more before she could convince him to get off her and attempt a phone call for help. My mother-in-law then had to secure medical attention for herself, as well as someone to provide supervision and transportation to Oakland for Grandpa. It was a real crisis situation. Throughout the course of his disease there were times he was combative and would physically injure and bruise her."

If this sort of situation developed in your family, who would intervene? Caregivers have limits. What are yours, and who will step in when you reach them?

At this point in your family conference, you might want to consider shared caregiving. Kaye Kepple and Diane Price are sisters whose mother, Marilee, had Alzheimer's disease. They lived two hundred miles apart, but wanting to provide home care for Marilee, their families worked out a shared care arrangement. Marilee spent one month with

70

Kaye's family in Palo Cedro, California, and the next with Diane's family in Sacramento. "Sharing responsibilities," Diane wrote, "gave us the breather we needed. My husband gave me ample opportunity to get away in the afternoon and evening when he could assume care of Mom." Is this a possibility for your family? It worked for Kaye and Diane until Marilee's peaceful death at home two years later.

Get a commitment from every family member to help in some way. Most important, is everyone willing to pray every day for you and their ailing relative? Can some of them help financially on a regular basis? Some families agree to reimburse the caregiver for her time, work, and restrictions.

"My dad's retirement income," said Glenn, "has been adequate so far to cover his needs and pay us the equivalent of nursing home room and board. My three sisters and I agreed to this arrangement before we started."

"We don't feel trapped and we are also reimbursed for his care," continued Glenn's wife, Carolyn. "Since caregiving keeps us from other jobs which we had planned, the family agreed that we should be reimbursed. I think this arrangement helps the others not to feel 'guilty' that we have Daddy's care while they each 'do their own things.' It also keeps me from feeling bitter, which I think might happen if the rest of the family had their freedom when we didn't. I would gladly do it for free if the others could take their turns. They are as capable as we are. But in lieu of that, being a paid caregiver is a good option for now. I think the financial burden is often great on top of all the other stress factors."

Some family members might agree to stay with your loved one while you get away for a while each week. Perhaps others can help with the sale, rental, cleanup, garage sale, or packing of your relative's house or apartment. Be sure someone takes responsibility for organizing, filling out, submitting, and keeping track of all of your loved one's health insurance forms, including Medicare. Try to have somebody besides the caregiver handle this mountain of paperwork, as it can be extremely time consuming.

71

Dean Price, who has exceptional talents for handling details, took care of all his mother-in-law's legal and medical bills. He made sure that all twenty-three doctors, hospitals, and clinics involved in her care were paid.

It is extremely important that all family members agree on the use of your dependent relative's money. This issue can be a loaded time bomb if it isn't discussed ahead of time. Defuse it before your conference ends. Designate one person to be the financial coordinator. This could be the caregiver, but more realistically it might be the person who investigated your loved one's finances.

Say, for example, that several of the adult children want to buy a television for Dad's room. Your family's financial coordinator, who knows how much money is available at a given time, should be consulted first. Then, before any purchase is made, he or she should make sure everyone else agrees with the purchase. Such an arrangement, set up verbally or in writing, streamlines decisions. And more importantly, it protects your vulnerable loved one against financial exploitation by relatives or friends.

Does everyone agree that your relative's Social Security pension be used for his or her welfare? If not, get that issue ironed out. Those funds are, after all, intended precisely for that. Your loved one will need special equipment, food, medicine, lights, water, gas, electricity, trash disposal, and much more. As time goes on he could need disposable diapers, special skin care, more medications, or even equipment to get him in and out of bed. Social Security is meant to make your relative, and your caregiving, as comfortable and easy as possible.

"My husband's mother received $333 per month from her Veteran's Widow's pension," shared a former caregiver. "We occasionally used some of this money for immediate needs, and the rest we saved for her funeral, for there had been no provision made to cover expenses when she died. We probably used $200 of her money the entire year she was here—for doctor's visits, medicines, and so forth. She has Blue Cross and Medicare."

This caregiver's job would have been far easier had she used some of that pension to hire a little help. Using your relative's resources to provide loving home care is not dishonest! It costs $1,800 to $3,000 a month for someone else to do what you are (or soon will be) doing. So why do untold numbers of caregivers refuse to take a penny for identical (and usually far better) care at home?

Your loved one worked and saved all his life for a rainy day. Now it's raining. Please put a protective umbrella over you both, and prayerfully use his or her money to provide the best possible care. And good care means that you, the caregiver, don't die in the process.

A week or so after your family conference, write a letter to everyone who came, as well as those who couldn't. Report on your relative's condition. Tell everyone how much their help and encouragement mean. Specifically thank each family member for what he or she promised to provide.

Preparing Yourself

We've talked about getting your loved one and your family ready for caregiving. Last, and most important of all, is preparing yourself for what is to come.

Spiritually

Spiritual preparation focuses your caregiving ministry, reminding you of your primary reason for doing it. Nothing will help you more than a daily time of prayer and Scripture reading. As you prepare, Psalm 139 will illuminate your caregiving path.

This soaring psalm lifts your heart to God's beauty, power, and holiness. Though often quoted as vibrant proof of the sanctity of unborn life, it has equal and poignant meaning for the aging and infirm. Caregiver and loved one alike could affirm: "If I say, 'Surely the darkness will overwhelm me, and the light around me will be night,' even the darkness is not dark to Thee, and the night is as bright as the day. Darkness and light are alike to Thee" (Psalm 139:11, 12).

73

Now look up this magnificent psalm and read it through twice. The first time, substitute your name for every pronoun. The second time, use your relative's name. For example, verse thirteen might read: "For Thou didst form Penny's inward parts; Thou didst weave her in her mother's womb."

As you twice whisper the Psalm, you will remind yourself at a deep level that there are two people intertwined in the caregiving equation: your loved one, and you. Both are equally precious in God's sight. But now one of you needs help from the other.

As you repeat this simple psalm/prayer, your heart will grow more tender toward your relative. You will be aware in your spirit that God has truly formed you both and loves each of you with an everlasting love. To paraphrase Psalm 139:16: "Thine eyes have seen Penny's unformed substance; and in Thy book they were all written, the days that were ordained for her, when as yet there was not one of them."

Mentally

Much has been said already about your mental preparation for caregiving. Read; listen; talk to others. Take advantage of every opportunity to learn your new task. Turn on your antenna right now for any and all books, articles, lectures, community college classes, symposiums, seminars, and workshops dealing with home health care and/or the disease afflicting your loved one.

Emotionally

It is almost impossible to emotionally prepare for caregiving in advance. Nothing can completely ready you for all that lies ahead: frustration, victory, fatigue, ongoing challenge, and satisfaction. This book was written to show you ways to cope with the emotional challenges you'll encounter.

Right now, as your caregiving starts, discipline yourself to take one day at a time, and no more. Plan for the unknown as much as you can. But live in today alone. Give it all you've got, and rest tomorrow in God's hands.

Practice thinking of yourself as a caregiver, accepting your new ministry.

Physically

Physical preparation isn't much different from what you've probably done most of your life. You need to eat a good diet low in fat and sugar, and especially high in energy foods like whole grains and complex carbohydrates. Also include lots of fresh fruits and vegetables.

Begin to exercise regularly, no matter how short the sessions are. For most caregivers, exercise is the first thing to go because they are too busy and too tired. Whatever you choose, make it something you really enjoy. Walking, gardening, or swimming are all wonderful tension relievers. Then try your best to participate in your activity three or four times a week.

Think through some of caregiving's nuts and bolts, and do everything you possibly can ahead of time. Have you decided where your loved one will live in your home? Will you need to add a wheelchair ramp or do any remodeling? Where will his equipment, when not in use, be stored? Have you thought and prayed about ways to make his or her room comfortable, warm, and welcoming? A room lovingly prepared gives ongoing affirmation of your relative's value and stature within the family.

"The need for proper equipment is essential," stresses Glenna Mills, the home health care consultant. "Special touches can make hospital equipment more homey and acceptable, such as colorful sheets on a hospital bed (a good Christmas gift for the patient). It also helps to use regular clothing that is easy to launder and put on. For example, sweatpants are nice looking, comfortable, and affordable."

If possible, talk to your relative about the things he or she would especially like around him: a treasured wing chair, yarn and knitting needles, a family gallery of pictures on one wall, cookbooks, a magazine stand, a small workbench, and so forth. As you pray for a sensitive spirit, God will bring to mind little things you can do to tell your loved one, "We love you, and we're so glad you're here."

Decide where and when your relative will have his meals. Some can be enjoyed all together as a family, but try to avoid his always eating with you. If you'll be gone, for example, he could have some meals in his room. Get him used to the idea of flexibility within the routine, that every meal won't be the same.

Think hard about what your loved one will do all day. Does he enjoy reading? Is there a library nearby? Would he enjoy listening to books on tape? Would an adult day-care center be a possibility? (More on these options in the next chapter.)

Last of all, be on the alert for a caregiver's support group for yourself, your family, and possibly your dependent relative. To locate one, call the social service departments of your local hospitals, check with nearby churches, phone the local chapter of the Alzheimer's Disease and Related Disorders Association, call the American Cancer Society, or contact other groups related to your loved one's illness.

Though every caregiving situation is different, support groups reach out to everyone involved. They meet regularly, offering inspiration and a safe, understanding place to deal with guilt. They allow you to share feelings, problems, successes, and failures. Most provide education, updates on medical information, housing alternatives, and some legal help. Best of all, a support group lets you know that no matter what's going on at home, you're not alone.

"Father, I feel overwhelmed .... Where do I start?"

"With one small step, beloved. I have gone before you."

"Even in this, Lord?"

"Even in this."

Chapter Five
Help!

When asked to describe her experience, a former caregiver was silent for several minutes. Finally, shaking her head slowly, she said, "That's so hard to do . . . it all sort of blends together."

She spoke for thousands of people who care. They plod through days and weeks and months and years. They smile at neighbors, vacuum rugs, wash sheets, and lug out trash cans. And they do most of it in a fog. Chronic exhaustion becomes the norm, seeping over their lives like mist on a lake. By time it is identified, it's a navigational hazard.

Yet most caregivers decline help, convinced they can do the job alone. If they can't, they feel sure they have failed. Those in the health-care field often expect near miracles of themselves. I know I did. When they can't do it all, their guilt may become even worse.

"To be honest," shared Mary Lou Sprowle, "I did not want 'outsiders' in our home. I still held to the philosophy of 'do it ourselves.' My husband, our daughter, and I did the job, but we really suffered for it in lost family times."

Your relative may loathe help as well, for entirely different reasons. For one thing, Mom may not have a clue about what her family faces in caring for her, and sees no need to have anyone but relatives assist her. Also, by accepting help, she admits that she needs it. And, as with most elderly or frail people, she may be highly suspicious of change.

Husbands, more than any other group, cling to old patterns. They often insist that nobody but their wife take care of them. The devoted but weary spouse of one man battling arthritis, strokes, and an aneurysm, sighed that he "*never* wants anyone but me to help."

You don't simply need relief. You don't simply deserve relief. You *must* have relief or the whole caregiving plan falls apart. Then where will Dad go? Accepting help reflects your commitment to caregiving. It is an act of love.

The kind and degree of help needed depends in large part on where you are in your caregiving season. If your loved one is still able to care for himself somewhat, you may need very little help now. But count on it: you are going to need more as time goes by.

"We brought her home to die," remembers one woman of her mother, "and that was four years ago!"

"We think it's essential to have some outside help," said Glenn Bradley after a few months of caregiving, "so we can do some things without my dad. Either a sitter or day care at a nursing home are possibilities."

"Get as much outside help as possible, and continue to work with care groups that will be able to relieve some of the emotional stress," urges Dayne Nix.

"If the caregiving is prolonged, the caregiver must find ways to get away from it for a few hours or days whenever possible, in order to keep perspective on his or her own life," emphasized Bob Pettit, whose mother's stroke left her paralyzed in one arm and unable to walk by herself. "Even with Mother in my sister's home, we couldn't believe how completely her problems had dominated our lives."

Do You Need Help?

Finding the right blend of help isn't like fixing an instant breakfast. You won't push a button and *presto!* It's all done. For one thing, caregiver resistance to stress differs greatly, depending on personality, age, health, cultural background, and previous caregiving models. Available financial resources also vary. The kind of help you need depends upon you, your loved one's condition, what's available in your community, and your caregiving budget. Answer the questions below to see if it's time to start looking for some assistance.

Are you physically unable to do something your relative's well-being requires—lift him, help him into a chair, or turn him over in bed? If you can't do what's necessary to care for your loved one because of your own size, health, or other reasons, you need help.

Are your friends giving you anxious glances? Are they asking things they never used to, like, "Are you *positive* you're all right?" Do you answer, "Sure" with a forced smile, when you're dying to scream "No"? Then you're not all right. You need help.

Is there certain caregiving behavior you're not proud of? Are too many of Aunt Lucy's meals cold? Are some of her medicines administered hours late, or maybe skipped altogether? If so, you're sailing perilously close to the shore of neglect. You need help.

Is there a painful gap between what your mind tells you about your loved one and what your heart feels? You know Dad can't help soiling his just-changed sheets. But as you strip his bed for the second time this morning, are you so angry you won't talk to him? The problem is not only Dad; it's you, too. You need help.

What Is Available?

Relief is out there, in every size and shape. "I have emotional support from friends and long-distance children," writes a working wife whose husband has Alzheimer's disease. "I also have one backup person to fill in occasionally, and a once-a-week person to be with my husband while I work late."

"During the morning we had a retired nurse who was a friend and wanted something to do part-time. She stayed through lunch," reported a working caregiver for both parents. "In the afternoon another friend came who was also a nurse with experience caring for elderly people."

Many retirees with health-related skills are eager to work part-time. Other caring help often comes from church friends and volunteers.

"A widowed lady from church befriended Mom and took her shopping and to her hair appointments," remembers Donajeanne Bogart. "She couldn't hear and Mom couldn't see, so it was an even trade. The church embraced Mom and became her social and extended family, several times a week."

Alert neighbors are frequently willing to help out in a variety of ways. If yours offer to lend a hand, by all means accept. Just don't overdo it. An hour or two a week should be maximum.

"We have two neighbors who will come for a few hours as sitters," reports Carolyn Bradley. "The family helps as they can. Don't be afraid to ask friends and neighbors for help," she continues. "Glenn's mother didn't have many friends help, but they didn't really know what she was dealing with and how much she needed help. Daddy's disease happened so slowly, most of the church wasn't really aware of his, or her, needs. People want to help if they know."

Teenagers, too, are eager for ways to earn extra money. Is a young person on your street willing to play cribbage or read to Dad an afternoon or two a week, so you can get away?

A huge group of health professionals is also standing by to assist you. Right now you may not need their services. But when you and your loved one clash over an area of care, you'll find that a trained professional may be able to solve the problem fast—which takes the heat off you.

When it comes to finding help, it's a good idea to focus on just one or two needs at a time—either your loved one's, or your own. Maybe Dad misses his buddies at the trailer park, the ones he used to watch football with. It's not the same at your house; you don't care who wins the game. All you want is some uninterrupted sleep, a little conversation with someone who makes sense, and time to plan that long weekend you and your husband promised yourselves. But for now it may be better to zero in on getting Dad around some people his age who share his interests. When he's happier, you'll feel more relaxed and creative as you make that long weekend happen.

But make sure your weekend away doesn't get put on indefinite hold. Wouldn't one of the wisest uses of Dad's Social Security and/or other resources be to provide some relief for you, his caregiver? Take a good look at your budget and begin saving for that weekend. Could you defer some other payment? Eat hot dogs and lentil soup twice a week? Can you hire someone to stay with Dad while you and your spouse spend two nights alone, somewhere else?

If your getaway doesn't look feasible at first, take a hard look at where the money's going. Call the person in your family who is the financial coordinator, if you have one. Talk it over. Search the budget and find a way. And remember that just as God knows your needs, He also knows your limits.

Don't overlook proper home health care equipment as another kind of help. You'll be amazed at what's available to make your job easier. Read the Yellow Pages under medical equipment and/or surgical appliances and supplies. Check department store and mail order catalogs. Many pharmacies may also have what you need. Some organizations, hospitals, and medical insurance groups keep durable medical equipment on hand to loan. Besides renting or buying, borrowing what you require is an option.

Give some thought to how often you would like extra help. Someone for an hour or two while you buy groceries? Someone twice a day, to help lift and turn your heavy patient? Someone to keep an eye on Dad several nights a week, so your sleep deficit doesn't reach the danger zone?

Each caregiving phase has different requirements. Prepare for continual adjustments. You'll no sooner establish a good blend of help when your situation or the condition of your loved one will change. Almost always, that means the kind of help you require will change, too. Train yourself to spot the end of one caregiving phase and the beginning of another. Then pray and plan ahead.

A word of warning: any help, as essential as it is, still invades your space. Your loved one is in your home with all her needs. Now here comes somebody else, asking all sorts of questions about Mom's bowel movements and whether or not she is capable of embroidering a pot holder. You'll use up valuable energy relating to both of these people, depleting what's available for your family. It may mean leaving the house when the help arrives, going elsewhere for the peace and quiet your home once provided.

Where Do I Start?

Begin your search for help the same way you start every other phase of caregiving: with prayer. "Everyone who asks, receives; and he who seeks, finds; and to him who knocks, it shall be opened" (Luke 11:10). Ask your heavenly Father to direct your efforts. He knows your heart and the heart of your loved one, and He will supply exactly what you both need.

Liz Cox, who provided home care for her mother for three and a half years, shares a good example of God's provision in this area. "One time in church," she remembers, "I sat next to a lady I didn't know. We began to talk and I was impressed to ask her if she would consider helping me care for my mother at night. She agreed and could drive, and the arrangement worked out fine. I believe the Lord provided help when I needed it."

As you pray and wait for God's provision, expect help to turn up in unexpected places at surprising times. One day Barbara Eagan was talking to a neighbor about her mother's inability to walk without two strong people on either side. Within days, she was supplied with a wheelchair from the Twin Peaks Senior Citizens Club. Not long afterward, a church member who is also a nurse helped the family locate a fully equipped hospital bed.

After you have poured out your heart in prayer, it's time to go shopping. Buy yourself a loose-leaf notebook with large center rings, lined paper, and dividers. Try to find one with pockets that will hold brochures and other loose information you'll accumulate. Keep looking until you find one you really like. This notebook is going to be your best friend throughout your caregiving season.

When Penny arrived at our home, John Patrick Gillese, a Canadian friend who is a writer and teacher, urged me to write down my experiences in caring for her. He also suggested I record any family history she shared, and her special memories. At first I resisted. How could mundane events like flannel sheets and cottage cheese salads be significant? But he insisted, and I started the process.

In the beginning I felt like a tube of biscuit dough—the kind you bang on a counter to open. The moment a tiny slit appears, the accumulated pressure inside pushes out the dough. Once I forced myself to put on paper what was happening in my life, I couldn't stop. My first entries went on for many pages, then settled down to one or two. Each time I made an addition to my journal I felt calmer.

The best part was reading what I had written months before, and realizing all that had happened. I had survived, and so had Penny. Journaling helped me keep the whole caregiving experience in perspective. When something awful happened, my journal encouraged me not to get too frantic. In caregiving, I learned, nothing is forever.

So select your notebook with care. You're going a long way together. When time allows, divide it into three sections. Label your dividers "Journal," "Caregiving Prayer Requests," and "Possible Sources of Help." On the first page of the journal section, write down all the reasons you chose to become a caregiver. Even if you had no choice, it's still important to write out how it all began. Take as long as you want and use as much space as you need. Be honest, especially about your feelings.

You'll review your reasons again and again, through tears and laughter. Your journal will become two things. First, it is a diary of an enormously significant part of two lives: your own and your loved one's. Second, it will provide visible proof of the mighty work that God is doing for both of you. Only one rule governs each journal entry: be truthful, even if you're ashamed of your feelings. Your honesty will become a tape measure of your progress.

The second section of the notebook is for caregiving prayer requests. Write down every need for help you think of, no matter how small or silly. Date each request and, at first, list the most urgent things at the top. Do you long to sleep uninterrupted for a whole night? Are you at the point where you need outside help? As you date and enter those needs in your prayer log, pray about them. Be as specific as possible about each entry. Review this list and pray about it as often as possible, because it will change.

Below each request, leave several lines to record God's provision for what you have asked. As months pass, your faith will move ahead by giant steps as you see His hand either remove the need or provide again and again exactly what you require.

The last section of your notebook will pinpoint every possible source of help for your situation. Begin by listing everyone in your family and what each person promised during your conference. If you couldn't manage a conference, but family members made written or phone promises, list them. Is each person doing what he or she agreed to do? Do you need to contact some of them?

If so, it will help to describe a typical day with their relative. Hunt for funny things to tell about, along with the serious ones. Show your family where problems exist, and why. Be specific about needing help in those areas. Whether you write, tape, or call, be sure to describe your own feelings. Facts are important, but your feelings are crucial.

Your family will be more involved if they know what's going on. You won't help by protecting them from unpleasant or sad developments: they deserve and need to know the truth. As your time and energy allow, periodic updates will bind all of you together.

After you set up your notebook, you need to master another essential caregiving skill: networking. Talk to neighbors, friends, doctors, ministers, or anyone who at some time cared for somebody. Find out how they managed, what helped, and what didn't. It won't take long to acquire a list of people and places to contact.

But keep in mind that all networks, whether made of threads, wires, or airwaves, work best when they allow two-way communication. Many caregivers forget that listening for information is as vital to their needs as speaking. Overburdened by their situation, they seize any opportunity to talk. Without intending to, they may monopolize conversations with narrow and often boring lists of problems. How can this be avoided? *Listen* to yourself.

Every caregiver needs to talk. The trick is to earn the right. Ask questions, listen for suggestions, and be genuinely interested in the other person—no matter how tired you are. Once active listening earns you a turn to speak, go to it. Share what's really going on, and what might make a difference. You've prayed about those needs. As you communicate them wherever you can, you'll receive answers.

SERVICE ORGANIZATIONS

In addition to relatives and friends, look for helpful community services. They may not offer everything you need, but you can find most of what you're looking for. The following services will have varying eligibility requirements and restrictions. Some will be at no charge, but many will ask for a full or sliding payment based on your relative's income.

(1) Adult Day Care

Trained supervisors in a homey group setting provide nursing services, which may include medications, social stimulation, nutritious meals, outings, counseling, ability-geared recreational activities, and physical therapy. Many hospitals, care centers, and nursing homes offer day care Monday through Friday and often on weekends, providing respite for round-the-clock caregivers. Most have waiting lists.

(2) Community Colleges

These facilities frequently offer excellent courses in basic home nursing and first aid.

(3) Home Health Services

These provide help with everything from registered nurse supervision to getting in and out of the tub.

(4) Homemaker and Chore Services

Such services provide assistance with household tasks, marketing, meal preparation, home repairs, and laundry for people alone all or part of the time.

(5) Hospital Social Workers

These people can furnish referrals, recommendations, and often the names of licensed professionals desiring employment full- or part-time. They offer tailor-made help if your relative is being discharged from the hospital.

(6) Housing Services

These help with maintaining or locating appropriate housing, including assisted living, senior housing apartments, licensed board and care homes, and retirement and life-care communities.

(7) Legal Assistance

This group of services offers help with everything from phone advice to representation.

(8) Nutrition Services

Contact this group if you need hot meals
served in an adult day-care center or delivered
to an adult in your home. In some areas, this
service may be available weekdays only.

(9) Respite Care

This service gives caregivers relief for a day,
overnight, or longer, through a variety of support functions.

(10) Telephone Reassurance

When people are alone, this service offers
friendly, regular telephone contact. Names
differ depending on the area: Ring-A-Day,
CareRing, Telecar, etc.

(11) Transportation and Escort Services

These provide public and private rides to
appointments, shopping, and recreation. Check
in your community for Dial-a-cab, Dial-a-bus,
Medicab, or some similar name.

Your local Area Agency on Aging (AAA) is the place
to begin your search for good outside services. Their federally funded, trained staff offers a variety of information
and community referrals for older adults, including
sources for many of the above. Most phone directories list
local Area Agencies on Aging. Or you can write them:
National Association of Area Agencies on Aging, 600
Maryland Ave. SW, Suite 208-W, Washington, DC 20024.
Or call (202) 484-7520.

PROGRAMS FOR FRAIL/OLDER PEOPLE

A number of organizations provide specific programs
for frail or older people, and for those who care for them.
Though many do not charge a fee, some do. You may find
help from one of the following:

(1) American Red Cross

The Red Cross teaches home nursing courses. Volunteers may also provide transportation and help with shopping.

(2) Churches and Other Service Organizations

Many offer volunteer programs including home delivered meals, telephone reassurance, chore and shopping help, and plain old visiting.

(3) Community Mental Health Centers

These offer counseling for all ages. Many conduct caregiver support groups.

(4) Departments of Social Services, Human Services, Public Assistance, or Welfare

In addition to Medicaid, these government agencies provide information on and assistance with many health and social services. Each differs, but in some states they may help locate equipment and provide chore service and other needs.

(5) Family Service Agencies

These nonprofit organizations offer many family services, such as counseling and respite care.

(6) Home Care Agencies

Through a variety of services, these agencies offer support programs for people of all ages, including care management, respite care, homemakers, chore services, nurse's aides, registered nurses, physical and occupational therapists, and instruction in skills that may be needed for some home-care situations.

(7) Hospice

Almost 2,000 local chapters provide, after a doctor's referral, support and care for dying persons and their families. Trained volunteers work with a professional team headed by the client's physician.

(8) Hospitals

The staff, especially social workers, arranges for help after a patient leaves the hospital. They also set up other referrals.

(9) National Council on the Aging (NCOA)

This national nonprofit organization provides a wealth of printed resources for older Americans and their families. For information about printed materials or membership, write: The National Council on the Aging, Inc., 600 Maryland Ave. SW, West Wing 100, Washington, DC 20024. Or call (202) 479-1200.

(10) Schools of Nursing

If one of these is in your area, its student nurses may be a part-time resource to help with your loved one's care.

(11) Senior Centers

These offer a variety of activities, possibly including recreation, transportation, education, hot meals, telephone reassurance, friendly visiting, counseling, legal services, organized group travel, and even help finding a job.

(12) Unions and Retiree Organizations

Groups such as the American Association of Retired Persons (AARP) may provide assistance or referral services.

(13) United Way

This organization may help with finances if the patient has no other sources of aid.

(14) Department of Veteran's Affairs

This may be another source of financial help for both short- and long-term care for veterans.

(15) Agencies pertaining to a specific disease

Organizations such as the American Cancer Society, National Federation of the Blind, Alzheimer's Disease and Related Disorders Association, Muscular Dystrophy Association, American Heart Association, or others your doctor may suggest are all potential sources of help. Many help obtain equipment. All provide some counseling and encouragement for patient and caregiver.

It is important to consider the resources on these lists as stepping-stones, not a yellow brick road to the Land of No More Problems. No book or person can plug a caregiver into the ideal help program. And as was stated earlier, your caregiver requirements are going to change based on your relative's ups and downs and your own needs. It's up to you to explore, phone, talk, and network.

Keep trying. If you hit a dead end, try something else. As nice as it would be, nobody is going to appear on your doorstep with a typed list of help options, phone numbers, and addresses. They are available, but you must be tough and persistent. It's up to you to find what's best for your situation.

When you launch your hunt for help, find a quiet hour when you won't be interrupted. Gather your caregiver notebook, pen or pencil, the newspaper's most recent want ads, and the phone book. Take a few minutes to ask God to lead your search. Then open your notebook to the third section, the one reserved for sources of help. Begin with a call to your loved one's doctor. Can he or she, or perhaps the office nurse, recommend a source of assistance?

Write down any suggestions you receive in your notebook: name, address, and phone number. Next, call each source. Introduce yourself, tell who referred you, and explain what you are looking for. If it's an agency or organization, write down the date of your call, the extension number and title of the person who helps you, the agency's working hours, the services offered, and the charge for each. Ask if there is a minimum service, such as two hours. Be sure to ask if they accept Medicare assignment or Medicaid if you have it. Also inquire about how they handle billing supplemental insurance.

Don't say good-bye until you either get some of your questions answered or a lead to something else. Thank the person, and explain that you'll get back to him later. It may be tempting to hire the first person or service you talk to, but don't. As with any other purchase, shop carefully and compare. You want to get the best possible service for your needs and your money.

Go right from one call to the next. You might also call your clergyman, who is trained to listen, encourage, and help. Next, check the newspaper want ads under "Positions/ Jobs Wanted." For now, simply enter the information in your notebook, leaving a few lines for notes when you make contact.

When you run out of referrals to call, pick up the phone book and turn to the first few white pages. Almost all areas of the country group their "Community Service" numbers together, as a public service. You'll find a wealth of resources to call, under such headings as counseling, emergency social services, health care services, housing, mental health, and senior services, to name a few.

Then try the Yellow Pages. Listings vary from one region to another, so try generic words: counselors, senior citizens, social and health services, hospice, home health services, nurses, nurses' registries, nursing homes, retirement, life-care homes and communities, day-care centers (adult), surgical supply houses, and attorneys' referral/ information service.

You'll also find listings, many which will overlap, in the white pages of your phone book under your state. For example, under "Washington, State of" are columns of various listings, such as "Social and Health Services, Department of." Also check white page listings under the names of your city and county.

Work out a plan to contact two or three of these services every day, entering each in your notebook. You'll be glad you took notes, because after ten or twenty calls the information blurs together. Keep at it and don't get discouraged. You're learning far more than you realize.

Not every service will provide what you need. Some won't offer what you're looking for, some will be too expensive, a few may be out of business. But keep networking, following up leads, dialing the phone, and taking notes. Sooner or later you'll make one or two contacts which will warrant an in-depth look.

"As complicated, confusing, and contradictory as government agencies and Medicare can be," suggests Ted Hutchinson, "a good word ought to be said for a system that (1) does provide excellent, skilled care and significant financial aid, and (2) physicians who are not getting rich, who work long, exhaustive hours, and who accept Medicare on assignment. (I think they deserve better.) Somehow we've lost sight of how far we've come, how much we have, and the good people who serve us. We have a lot of help that was unavailable to previous generations, and we ought to be more thankful."

Your biggest need at the moment may be a transfer bench, so Mom can sit down while she bathes. Or maybe, as happened to Penny one summer, a major need is transportation. Her bridge broke, and after a home visit our dentist said the equipment to repair it was in his office. After many calls, dead ends, and considerable networking, we discovered our city's wonderful Spokane Area Special Transportation (SASTA). With twenty-four hour's advance notice, one of a 35-van fleet arrived at our front door. A trained and cheerful driver wheeled Penny to the van's hydraulic lift and, once inside, safely secured her wheelchair. Penny's delight at having a bus ride dwarfed the dentist's repair job. The excursion cost $1.20 per person. Round-trip.

Locating reliable transportation for your loved one is vital. So are transfer benches and hand-held shower heads. But most of the help you need will probably be in the form of living, breathing people. And before you let anyone into your home, much less do anything for your relative, you need to screen them. This is a must, whether the person stays with Dad for an hour or helps with his care seven days a week.

"Be *very* selective in hiring help," warns Renée Kuehl, who hired full-time and part-time help during her mother's three-year illness. "Follow up on references. Check on the person's routine often."

Help provided by a Home Health Agency will do much of the screening for you. And if your regular person gets sick, they'll send a substitute. But you should still ask the agency's supervisor about their hiring standards, because these may vary widely—even within the same city. Has the person they suggest had prior experience? Is he or she licensed, or certified? By whom? Does the agency provide its employees Workman's Compensation, malpractice, and/or liability insurance? Do agency employees carry additional liability insurance?

Once these questions are answered to your satisfaction, but before you reach any agreement, try to meet the person suggested by the agency. (Occasionally there will be a charge for the time required for such a meeting.) Read on for suggested questions you may want to ask this person. If you are not pleased, ask the agency to send someone else.

Before hiring nonagency help, check with your insurance company about your homeowner's (or renter's) policy. What sort of liability and guest medical insurance does it provide? Do you need more? If your nonagency help will work twenty or more hours a week for you, ask your legal adviser about your state's requirements regarding Social Security and Workman's Compensation. Ask if you or your relative need the protection of bonding for employees.

Although you may locate help through the newspaper's want ads, you could run your own advertisement. Be sure your ad makes clear any special requirements, such as non-smoking or elderly experience. Your ad might read:

```
Wanted: experienced,licensed
nurse's aide. Part-time, to help
with elderly patient. Must be
able to lift. Competitive wages.

Call 555-1234, evenings.
```

Screening Steps

When you do locate someone who may meet your needs, here are some screening steps. If the person is sent by an agency, you will not need to ask all the questions.

Step #1

Conduct a preliminary screening by phone. Ask for a minimum of two references. Get more if possible. If it matters to you, ask if the applicant smokes. Is he or she licensed? May you see the license? Does he or she drive? What does the applicant charge per hour? Ask about everything else important to you, such as the person's ability to assist a large, partially paralyzed man. Don't limit yourself to questions that require only yes or no. Make them open-ended, such as "What things do you enjoy about home nursing?"

Step #2

Tell the applicant you'd like to check the references, and say that you will get back in touch.

Step #3

Phone every reference, first introducing yourself and asking if the time is convenient. Ask how long the applicant provided care for the reference. What was the nature of the care? Was lifting a problem? Verify the pay rate quoted to you. Was the person pleased with the care? Was the applicant honest? Reliable? Did he or she miss many days, whatever the reason? What were his or her strengths? Weaknesses? How did the reference obtain the applicant's help? Would the reference rehire the applicant? Was the person on time? Professional in appearance? Did he or she take initiative? Was he or she an adequate cook? Verify all information the prospective employee gave you. Is everything you were told true? Thank the reference for his or her time. Leave your phone number in case the person thinks of other information you should know.

Step #4

If you are satisfied with the references' responses, invite the applicant to your home to meet you and your relative. Schedule this during the day, if possible, and ask the person to bring his or her license. Pay attention to little things. For instance, does he or she show up alone? Is someone waiting in the car? (Not good.) Does he or she smell like smoke, and would this upset you or your loved one? Then walk through the routine you need help with. Verify, again, the rate of pay. Look carefully at the license. Is it current? (Any license could, of course, be invalid or fraudulent. But such cases are unusual, and careful checking eliminates many hiring errors.) Promise to get back to the person. When you do hire someone, start out on a trial basis until you're certain everyone is satisfied. Write out your basic employment agreement, sign it, and have your employee do the same.

After you've screened some applicants and hired one of them, remember that people come with names, families, good and bad days, aches and pains, missed lunches, and wet shoes. Though highly recommended, licensed, bonded, and insured, the person who arrives at your door to help won't look like an angel of light. She may look like Opal Gladstone.

Maybe Opal has bunions, and today they hurt. Maybe Opal has three grown children who all live at home. One is unemployed, and none helps buy groceries or pay the rent. Probably Opal has a God-given love for the elderly and sick. But Opal may tend to talk too much. And perhaps she thinks clocks are for decoration.

You need to get ready for Opal before she arrives on your front porch thinking about her bunions. Begin by making a list of emergency names and phone numbers, including your loved one's doctor, nurse, aide, agency if you have one, ambulance, family members, and your minister or priest. Leave this list near your phone.

Next, make a realistic assessment of the main things you'd like Opal to do. What she does will depend in part on how long she's there. Prepare a written list, with the things you'd most like her to do at the top. Jot down two or three extra little jobs, in case Opal works fast. Rework this list until it suits you, then copy it so Opal can read it.

After Opal arrives, show her where to hang up her raincoat. Introduce her to your relative. Then, one by one, go through everything on your list with her. Show her where to find whatever she'll need, and how things work. Set out soap and a clean towel, so she can wash her hands. Be ready to answer questions. Many willing helpers flounder because the caregiver neglects to figure out just why they are there.

When Opal goes to work, stay around for five or ten minutes. But don't keep talking to her. Give her time and space to do her work without feeling watched. You may be nervous and not want to leave your relative. Or you may be so eager to escape that you slept last night with the car keys under your pillow. No matter how you feel, give Opal a few minutes to figure out how the vacuum cleaner works and which cat stays outside.

When you're satisfied the roof's going to stay on, *leave.* Drive, walk, go with a friend, or take a bus. But get out. It will do you more good than you can imagine, and it will be a lot better for Opal and Dad. It's terribly hard to do this when you've been the whole caregiving show, but you'll learn—in about four minutes. Practice forgetting your relative, his care needs, and everything going on at home. Dad and Opal will probably get along fine. And you'll begin to reel in some parts of your life you thought got away.

After you go back home and Opal leaves, keep a few things in mind. Remember that you'll never clone yourself. You may have built up Opal's abilities far beyond reality. Did she do what you asked? Was it well done? Was it so awful you never want to see her again? If she's from an agency, should you call her supervisor and report her? If she's not from an agency, should you write or call your local Area Agency on Aging?

Are you certain you communicated what you wanted Opal to do? Did she understand? How was her attitude? How did Dad accept her? Most important, are you better off now than before she came? Why or why not? Unless you have twenty-four hour help, whoever comes in eventually goes out. You're on duty the other twenty-two or twenty-three hours. No matter how hard Opal tried, she's not Wonder Woman.

Would you like Opal back again? Would you like to set up a regular weekly visit from her? If so, why not call Opal or her agency right now, and arrange a time for her next visit? That way you can look forward to it. Even if it's just for an hour or two, Opal's job means the end of yours—for a while, at least. As short as the relief is, it's better than what you had before. Keep in mind that Opal is your gift to yourself—and indirectly, to Dad.

But be on the alert. Dad may well be allergic to Opal. He probably likes the same routine, mealtime, furniture arrangement, and caregiver. He has come to expect consistency week in and week out.

Penny often criticized people who came to visit or help. She usually waited until they left, though several times she smiled at one of our regular nurse's aides, saying, "We won't be needing you today." Penny, like countless others, resisted help. To accept it meant she wasn't well, that things weren't the way they had always been. Penny didn't want help. She wanted me. No matter how tired I was, I wasn't the help. I was her daughter-in-law, "giving her a hand"—and preserving her illusion of a still-normal life.

Your loved one may make up some terrible things Opal did, but don't be too quick to call Opal's supervisor. Give her a chance. Dad doesn't want her. Dad wants you. And he'll do just about anything to keep you handy. If you think Dad's embroidering the truth a bit, but you don't know what to do, jump ahead to Chapter 8. Then set up another visit from Opal.

When you do find people who meet most of your needs, take good care of them. "Give support to your help," urges Renée Kuehl. "Surprise them with little gifts. Compliment them." As time goes by, become sensitive to what's going on in *their* lives. Remember holidays and special events in small ways.

You prayed for someone to help. But God didn't send a white knight. He sent Opal. She may not be quite what you expected, but she *is* making things easier. And it's just possible that God sent her into your home and life for more than your loved one's bath. It's no longer only you and Dad. It's you, Dad, and Opal. And God deeply loves all three of you.

"I need help, Lord, but I feel so bewildered . . . ."

"My ways are not your ways, my child. Reach out, and don't be afraid. I am at work in all of your lives."

"Even in this, Lord?"

"Even in this."

Chapter Six

Do We Have to Take This Road, Lord?

It was almost eleven when Bob got home from a long evening meeting. He changed into his pajamas and a robe, then opened our bedroom door. "I'll be right back," he told me in a low voice. "I want to see if Mom's thirsty."

I nodded, worried about the fatigue in his eyes. I heard him gently open Penny's door. He checked on her every night, but rarely this late.

"Wha . . . what . . . ." Her voice quavered with fear.

"It's okay, Mom. It's Bob."

"Bob?"

"Yes. Mom, do you want any water?"

"What?"

"Do you want any water?" I could tell he was bending over her bed.

"Why are you asking me that?"

"I just thought you might want some."

"Don't you have any water in the house?"

"Yes. I just wondered if you were thirsty."

"What?"

When Bob finally got back to our room we managed to laugh, though his face was pale with weariness. We get up at five in the morning, and he needed every minute of sleep he could get. But Penny's confusion and poor hearing had stretched what should have been a thirty-second conversation to ten minutes. In the process, Bob's caregiver frustration level climbed another notch.

So did mine as the months went by. I'm a creature of habit and like to do things quickly so I can move on to something else—usually something more interesting. So when Penny first joined us, I sought a routine. *Just like a newborn,* I had thought, *ease her into a schedule and before long things will run like clockwork.*

Wake her up between seven and eight. Bed bath, breakfast, make bed. Medications. Short visit. Help into recliner. Daily paper and glasses. Lunch. Short visit. Television on "Perry Mason." Television off for snooze. Change diaper and nightie. Brush and rearrange hair. Short visit. Serve dinner. Help into bed. Read Bible. Short visit. Pray. Lights out.

Some days the schedule worked out like that, but more often it didn't. One day she vomited her breakfast. Another time she had leg cramps and needed a heating pad and massage. I never knew what would derail my carefully prepared plans.

One memorable day the traveling hairdresser arrived for Penny's twice-monthly shampoo. Penny hated having her long hair washed from the day she arrived, and I had quickly decided that was one area I would avoid at all costs. She glowered at the beautician, then braced her hands on the bathroom walls as she was wheeled into it, insisting she was not having her hair washed. The frazzled hairdresser came to get me.

When I walked into Penny's room she pointed at the woman and said loudly, "Look at her. She looks funny! I'm not having my hair washed!" The helpless attendant stood to one side, shifting the brush and comb from hand to hand.

Tired, exasperated, and angry that anyone in our house would be insulted, I lost my temper. I informed Penny she would most definitely have a shampoo, and I personally wheeled her into the bathroom. Then I ran down the hall, into the backyard, and rushed next door to our neighbor, Edith. She listened to my tale of woe, hugged me, and poured me a cup of coffee. Penny ended up with shining clean hair, but I was so upset it threw my whole day off.

Dependent relatives have one set of plans; caregivers have another. The two people may appear to move ahead on the same road, but collisions are only a matter of time. Busier than she's ever been in her life, the caregiver rushes through each hour. Everything she does is important. She dashes here and there, lugging along the beloved domestic and professional parts of her previous life. And one by one she piles on new caregiving demands: no-added-salt diets, two-hour bath procedures, endless phone calls, and much more.

She struggles through each day, always trying to complete more jobs in less time. But as she speeds up, her loved one's world slows down. Mom wants and needs to talk. She can't stand the new therapist and complains about it every eight minutes. Dad longs to go for a stroll.

"We need to hurry a little today, Dad. I've got to get to the bank."

"You're always going somewhere. What's the rush?"

The caregiver laughs, but her stomach knots.

David Sprowle thought caregiving would be a positive experience. "I thought Mom would fit in with the family," he said, "but it never worked out like I thought it would. My sisters were not mentally ready to do the job. One lives away; the other two are in a world of their own. So I was it."

Not all collisions between your plans and your relative's will be traumatic. Sometimes you'll find yourself laughing.

"I started a little Monday morning cleaning today," Nancy Jo Moore told her dad, who is going blind.

"Why are you cleaning?" her indignant father wanted to know. "I did it last year!"

But more often you are likely to feel like another former caregiver who remembers the impact on her daily routine when her husband's mother lived with them for a short while. "After our eight year old left for school," she said, "I used to go shopping and do whatever else was needed. But Mom had a broken shoulder, a fractured pelvis, and was in lots of pain. She slept until ten every morning, and I just waited for her to wake up. Then she wanted to shower and dress, and of course needed help with everything. By the time she did all that and I fixed her breakfast, it was past noon. Then she was so fearful and helpless, I never went out. I shopped in the evenings, after my husband got home. It was easier than living with the guilt of leaving Mom alone."

She recalls hushing her little boy and his friends as they played. "Mom couldn't stand any confusion," she explained. "Not even the boys' laughter." This mother's personal and family plans collided with her relative's needs many times a day.

Mary Lou Sprowle remembers that the hardest part of caregiving was "the everyday sameness, confinement, and her soon acquired 'Queen-for-a-Year' attitude. I wanted to be a good servant, but I grieved for myself and my life that was shoved back behind her expectations daily."

Some caregiver-patient collisions are total. "As the childishness increased," wrote Barbara Eagan about her mother, "it has been hard and rather nerve-racking to see her constantly hit her silverware against her glass, play with her food, etc. She went through a long period of tapping her hand on whatever was available. She also turned every knob she could reach; we became concerned about the gas cookstove. I hid all of the matches and candles, but later she got hold of a picture album and started to use the scissors on it. I went through the house again collecting all of the scissors or any other items I thought might be harmful."

Barbara continued, "My father still drives Mother to the beauty shop once a week to have her hair done, though he takes total, 24-hour care of her. It got to the point where he was setting the alarm for every three hours through the night to take her to the bathroom. But even with this method he was still not able to keep her dry."

Barbara's father, Ted, is retired. He cares for his wife all day, every day, but still makes some plans for himself. "It is difficult to be confined and not able to be gone from home longer than a couple of hours," he states. "Dressing and undressing her continues to be more difficult. Many times I get very little cooperation when I am trying to get her arms in and out of sleeves and her legs in and out of pants. It does take patience. Her ability to use eating utensils is also becoming less efficient. Seventy-five percent of the time I have to feed her. She has had diarrhea a number of times—on the bed, rug, floor, etc. It is frustrating. The added laundry keeps me busy trying to keep up-to-date."

Jane Hutchinson is the mother of three small children. Her mother-in-law, Janet, has senile dementia, and requires help with almost everything. Jane's plans for each day are endless. So are Janet's needs. When Janet first moved in with them, Jane wrote, "All of a sudden this totally independent woman needs it all. I think a bedpan will be a must! She needs help with even basic things like a bed bath and brushing her teeth." Jane added that, "My feelings and fears are probably accentuated by my monthly cycle and the fact that my two year old has chosen to assert his level of individuality very brazenly during the past few days. This is mostly evidenced by a tilt of his chin and a hearty 'no' when told to do something."

Fifteen months after caregiving began, Jane shared that "My mother-in-law gave me quite an interrogation: Who are all these children? Who is the Mom? Who are *you* married to? She seemed pleased at the end of it all. An hour later she was sobbing and hostile, and ate dinner in bed. Another hour later, all was well. You never know. I talked to Mom about seeing the doctor (because she was crying so often), and she got furious. She flat refused, saying she'd tell the world what we're doing to her!"

When Penny first joined our family, the most difficult part of her care centered around her physical needs. Because she was incontinent, at least partial daily baths were a must. My energy drained to the last drop as I rolled her from side to side, helped her sit up, and reassured her as I lowered her, shrieking, into a chair.

But it wasn't long before we encountered a part of her care that was even more challenging. Dr. Joan Craig, my doctor who agreed to also care for Penny, diagnosed her condition as "organic brain syndrome." Its symptoms included no memory and disorientation to time, place, and person. We were soon introduced to one characteristic of senile brain function, at least for Penny—probable transient ischemic attacks (TIA's).

Her attacks began abruptly and had no predictable interval. Sometimes months went by between them. Sometimes only a week. But we knew immediately when one had taken place. Penny became unnaturally talkative. She heard people singing. She repeated over and over that she needed to get dressed. She demanded her cane "so I can walk." She rang her call bell a dozen or more times an hour. She asked for her bra, hose, and girdle. (After several tries, we had eliminated tight clothing because it bothered her.)

After one TIA she tugged at the tray of her chair, which was kept locked over her lap for her protection. She jerked it back and forth so hard the noise could be heard all over the house. She pulled every hairpin out of her hair. She asked continually if Bob were all right, and why wasn't he here, and what had happened to him? Normally eager to get to bed as early as possible, she refused to go until ten or eleven at night.

During one episode we wheeled her into the family room for dinner. "I heard them singing out there," she announced, pointing to the backyard. Next she peered into the oven, "What are you cooking? Have you locked all the doors in the house?" At the end of the day she gave several of our new outdoor chairs to a nurse's aide, who politely declined the gift.

Penny's agitation always escalated after a TIA. The worst night occurred a few months after she arrived.

Around four A.M. on a weekday morning, a strange thump in her room startled me awake. I rushed across the hall to find Penny slumped on the edge of her bed, her legs dangling through the bars of the side rails, her nightgown unsnapped, pins out of her hair, and a soiled diaper on the floor. She had tried to clean herself with the water in her drinking glass, now spilled. The lamp lay sideways on the floor, turned on. By time I waded through the cleanup, Penny had gratefully gone back to sleep. I couldn't.

All that day her needs for reassurance and help, not to mention hygiene, collided head-on with my own plans. I dragged through shopping and desk work, enjoying neither. I was exhausted, yet with every episode Penny needed extra encouragement to eat, which took additional time. She required endless repetitions. But even the explanations caused problems, because she denied their reasons.

"It isn't safe for you to walk, Penny. We're afraid you might fall and hurt yourself."

"There's nothing in the world wrong with me. Give me my cane and I'll show you."

Back to square one. Our mutual frustration took many forms, some hilarious. One late summer afternoon the nurse's aide helped Penny onto the commode. The aide called me a short time later because Penny refused to get up. I spent fifteen minutes talking, coaxing, and joking as I tried to humor her up and off. Finally, laughing, I told Penny it was going to be a long night sitting there.

"You don't want to spend the night on the commode, do you, Penny?"

"I'm not on the commode!"

By the time the aide and I finally combined forces to pry her off, it was dark outside.

Incidents like this one continued despite medication. During them, I grasped a basic fact I should have comprehended long before: Caregiving can't be compartmentalized.

I still had my own life. I still made plans and hoped to carry them out. And I still wanted to care for Penny. I had expected to be able to do both if I organized, streamlined, and planned every detail. I thought her care would fit into my cherished routine. I was wrong. Detailed planning helped, but it wasn't enough. Right from the start, Penny's needs eclipsed my plans on an almost daily basis. The only variable was whether the eclipse was partial or total.

Another caregiving area that demanded surprising amounts of my time was occupational therapy. Unless Penny had recently undergone a TIA, she sat for hours staring into space. I found myself endlessly concerned that she was bored. I knew my concern was irrational, but I still worried. We had moved her out of her house into ours, and I feared we had let her down.

Most of her days blended into a predictable sameness, and I felt guilty. One day I discovered her watching "Challenge of the Gobots," a cartoon with orange and purple space monsters grunting at each other. I snapped it off, mortified that her life had come to this.

I racked my brain for things she might enjoy. I brought folded squares of fabric and spools of thread for her to handle, remembering the dress shop she owned. I checked out fashion and family magazines with lots of pictures from the library and encouraged her to read them. We took every visitor to her room for a chat, something she enjoyed. I bought tiny gifts for her to wrap and give to neighbors, arranging pre-cut squares of wrapping paper and ribbon beside them on her tray. She could not even begin the task. Still I kept trying . . . and worrying.

Care facilities hire round-the-clock staff for every level of care—people who work eight hours and leave. But home caregivers have no respite. They are on duty until the need for caregiving ends. Is it possible for a caregiver and dependent relative to meaningfully coexist on the same road? In many ways, yes. Let's talk about four steps you can take to ensure continuation of your own life.

Back Away from the Problem

It's usually many months before a new caregiver comes up for air. But as soon as you find a free hour, it's an enormous help to mentally back away and survey what's going on.

When you assume responsibility for someone else, your own life gets pushed aside. What's the normal reaction to that? You probably get tense, rushing faster and faster, chasing the tail of an elusive system always beyond your grasp. That kind of tension forces you to demand more and more of yourself as you race against the clock.

The flip side of your long-distance dash is your loved one's inability to hurry. Dad doesn't hear the tick of your time clock. He wants to talk, to watch football together, to regain some measure of control over his life. And even if he wants to hurry because he senses you do, he probably can't. Dad's at a place in his life where hurry is past tense.

Realistic Assessment

Once again, the solution begins with prayer. Find a quiet half hour, longer if you can squeeze it from your day. Ask the Lord to help you take an honest look at your loved one's daily needs—and your own. The greatest help will come if you do this with an attitude of whispered, yielded prayer.

"Lord, help me see things from Mom's viewpoint. Help me feel what it's like to open my closet and not recognize the clothes. Show me how I can help her pick out her own outfit in spite of this. And, Father, please show me how much time she really needs."

Go on this way, step by step, through your loved one's day. Take a hard look at the time you need to prepare her special meals, do extra loads of her wash, drive to the pharmacy and surgical supply house, and take Mom to her doctor. Present every detail before your heavenly Father.

Next ask God to give you fresh insight into your own life. Yield your plans and agenda to Him—all of it, even the secret dreams. Ask the Lord to open your spirit to changes He wants to make in your life and in the life of your loved one. Then resume your day, confident that He has heard and is working in your specific situation.

Flexibility

After your time of prayer, it won't be long—perhaps only a day or two—that you'll begin to realize how much time your relative's care really demands. When Penny moved in, I told myself that the bulk of her daily care should only take about an hour. When I assessed it step by step in prayer, I discovered it would require at least twice that—longer if she didn't feel good or was cross. Although I wasn't happy about that, it helped to squarely face facts.

I gained new insight by examining Jesus' life, studying the pattern of His days. He, too, had destinations, plans, and goals. But in the midst of them, He was open to the stops and changes along each day's road.

Once, as He rushed toward the home of Jairus' dying daughter, a women who had been hemorrhaging for twelve years touched the hem of His garment (Matthew 9:18-22). Rather than asking His disciples to exercise more efficient crowd control, Jesus stopped, turned around, and spoke to her. In what had to be the most wonderful news of her life, He told her that her faith had made her well. Then He continued to Jairus' house. That weak, pale woman interrupted Jesus' plans for the day. But He was willing to set aside His own agenda and minister at her point of need.

Following Jesus' example of flexibility, I tried building a cushion of time around my caregiving. My evaluation told me that Penny's personal care would require about two hours, so I planned for three. I slowly came to grips with the fact that caring for Penny meant losing most of my morning. I had tried to rush around and deny that fact, but it hadn't worked. What did work was surrounding her care with a time cushion. This system diffused much of the tension and anger I had previously experienced from post-poned jobs and plans.

As time passed, I learned to avoid anything in my day that could conflict with special appointments in Penny's. When the R.N. was scheduled for her monthly physical assessment, when our minister planned to visit and pray with her, or when the surgical supply house was to deliver another egg crate mattress, I blocked out my calendar for the afternoon. Afterward, if time allowed an errand or two, fine. But if it didn't, that was fine, too.

I also learned to pad other chores related to Penny with extra minutes. It wasn't easy. I'm goal-oriented, and putting on the brakes comes hard. But before long I learned to make time to sit down with her for a mini-visit after I put away her clean laundry. Two or three minutes chatting about anything satisfied Penny. I enjoyed it, too. The secret was padding each day with that cushion of time. Other things ran more smoothly as Penny reflected my lack of hurry.

"We have learned we must be extremely flexible," wrote Glenn Bradley. "No two days are alike. We can never count on getting a good night's sleep. We try to plan with enough slack to accommodate changes. If we couldn't bend, we would break."

Another big boost toward caregiver flexibility came when I learned to set realistic (rather than idealistic) daily goals. As Bob and I talked about what each of us wanted from our evenings at home, we decided to divide and conquer. We learned to share Penny's before-bed care and develop an organized system we could both count on. Our goal was to enjoy some free time with each other.

We agreed that he would set out her pills each night, put her to bed, and stock her upper closet on weekends with diapers and liners. I would cook her meals, do her wash, and take care of appointments, errands, and phone calls related to her care.

Penny rarely ate dinner with us because she liked to go to bed very early. After she finished eating in the family room and announced she was tired, Bob wheeled her back to her room. After helping her into bed, he read to her from the Bible and prayed with her.

During that time, I enjoyed listening to the news as I fixed our own dinner. As months and years passed, this system worked. The more we streamlined Penny's routine care, the easier things became.

We both found it important to prayerfully evaluate our outside commitments. It didn't take a genius to figure out that Penny's care demanded much of our energy. We knew we needed more rest, so we weeded out certain activities and made others we especially enjoyed a high priority.

One caregiver, whose husband has Alzheimer's disease, wrote that one of the things that helped her most was "dropping excess baggage such as unnecessary commitments, responsibilities, and self-appointed expectations."

Diane Price urges caregivers: "Get enough rest. Make this possible by giving up activities that you can resume after caregiving is over."

I discovered that the only extras my day would tolerate were a couple of errands, attending a Bible study, or going with Bob to a friend's house for dinner. Notice that word *or*—not *and*. If I tried to crowd in too much, I ended up tired and irritable. This was a hard lesson. It was like cutting booster rockets that had always burned brightly, whatever the day held.

Many other caregivers make the same discovery. Diane wrote: "I've always been active, so this was a complete change. My husband and I still had a limited social life because we shared Mom's care with my sister and were able to vacation. Our lives became more *structured*, but as strange as it may seem, eliminating some of our organizational activities had its good points."

It took practice to slowly separate our lives from Penny's, but we got better at it. For a caregiver, that separation can never be total. We learned to include her in events that were natural and easy and meant something to her. But if friends arrived for dinner when she was already in bed, we let her sleep while we enjoyed our guests.

I took advantage of every possible shortcut. If there was a faster or easier way to do one of my caregiving jobs, I grabbed it. I prepared food Penny liked, such as meat loaf, in quantity. Then I divided it into small portions and froze them. I bought vitamins and pills in bulk to minimize shopping.

Try to involve your loved one in his or her own care as much as possible. For example, Jane keeps a calendar in her mother-in-law's room. In the large squares for each day, she writes "shampoo" or "bed change" in bright letters and sticks a smiling face on the day a task is finished. She says that this "gives Mom a sense of things happening in her life."

If your relative is confused about where things are or what they do, label the drawers, cupboards, and appliances. Group similar outfits together, on one hanger if possible, to encourage easier clothing choices. Be sure to talk about meals: what you're planning, what your loved one would enjoy, and favorite flavors of ice cream, for example.

Wherever he or she eats, vary the place mat and dishes. Arrange a tiny bouquet of flowers in season, unless you're afraid they'll be eaten along with the salad. Decorate for every holiday you can think of. Each year Penny had a Christmas tree, complete with twinkle lights, balls, and a star. It sat on her dresser, where she could see it from any place in her room. Celebrate small things, like the first snowfall or spring tulip. When our daughters Ann and Leslie visited, they often sat beside her to knit, look at photo albums, or simply visit. Seize every opportunity to say "we love you" in many ways.

Don't forget to talk with your relative about doctor's appointments, upcoming birthdays, graduation gifts for children or grandchildren, or anything out of the ordinary about to happen. Even if the information is soon forgotten, your loved one is involved for those few shining moments.

Relinquishment

After you've prayed, assessed, organized, streamlined, and involved your relative in everything you can think of, you will come to the place of caregiver relinquishment You are giving the best care you know how to give. Now it is time to let go. Your loved one is there, and your life must move around him. Not over him. Not in the opposite direction. You must move around him—and on.

God is at work in your relative's life, and He is power-fully at work in yours. He is teaching you lessons you could perhaps learn no other way. He is showing you what has eternal value in your life and what doesn't. God is refining you, and that process hurts.

As Bob and I prayed through every part of our care-giving, our understanding and love for Penny grew—even on the days we felt like running away . . . even during her most unlovely, most negative times. And after a heart-to-heart talk with Dr. Craig, I was able to relinquish my guilt about Penny's activities. She told me that "the price she pays for living in your home is a lower level of stimulation."

We didn't have thirty activities a month at our house. We didn't have visiting glee clubs or embroidery classes. Home care is never perfect. Time hung heavily on Penny's hands. Her horizons were sometimes near and boring. But beating in our hearts was the conviction that Penny didn't care. She wanted so much to be with us, and we wanted her to be there (even if that meant she sometimes watched "Challenge of the Gobots"). I hadn't failed as a play thera-pist, after all.

Gethsemane and Other Roads

There was something about Jesus few people could resist. Men well-launched into careers as fishermen, tax collectors, and tentmakers dropped everything when He called their names. Some left wet fishing nets lying on the white sand in tangled piles. Others wedged forgotten tax records in the sturdy limbs of sycamore trees. The Master beckoned. They followed.

Much caregiving is similar. We listen for His call, His direction. He is irresistible, and we desire no other. But like those men so long ago, we cannot see where He leads us. The journey's end lies hidden from our sight.

For His early followers, traveling with Jesus was fun at first. They camped beside the Sea of Galilee, slept under the stars, and helped Him distribute fish and bread to vast crowds of hungry people. In our homes today, we enjoy arranging our relative's room and preparing favorite foods. We pray for sensitivity, patience, and wisdom. We ask Jesus to teach us little ways to serve, ways to reflect His mighty love.

But as our relative's steps falter, the journey grows more difficult. It helps to remember that Jesus' campsite under the stars led to Gethsemane. And Gethsemane led to the crown of thorns, and scourging, and a splintered cross dragged through the crowded, noisy streets.

Lord, I want to travel this road with You, but it's steeper than I thought. I'm caring for my husband, Lord, trying to let You love him through me. But it's getting hard. I'm so tired, Lord. When I started out it seemed manageable. I didn't know then it would lead into this valley, where the thorns along the way pierce like knives. Must I come this way to follow You? Could I take another road?

Jesus longed to avoid the agonizing journey from Gethsemane to Golgotha. When He prayed about it, His sweat became as great drops of blood. He asked, "Father, if Thou art willing, remove this cup from me; yet not My will, but Thine be done" (Luke 22:42). Even as He dreaded what was to come, He yielded His life to the Father's will.

Caregiving sets aside our own lives to a great extent. It denies much that we have longed for and looked forward to. We look back, remembering how good life once was, as Jesus did. We look ahead and cannot help but be afraid, as He surely was.

And sometimes caregivers must take another road. The task may drain strength and spirit until other arrangements become essential. But until that time comes, no caregiver should be surprised when her road leads to places of acute pain. That is the nature of caregiving.

Jesus was spat on, insulted, and ridiculed. Because of Him, we can bear the same if necessary. His gentle voice has called us, and we dropped our nets and followed. He is with us on the road, even when we can't feel His presence. He is with us in the undeserved anger, and in the times of sullen silence.

"I feel as if there's a detour sign on my life, Lord. I can't see where I'm going . . . ."

"Listen for My voice, precious one. I am leading the way."

"Even in this, Lord?"

"Even in this."

Chapter Seven
All This, and Hot Flashes, Too

Eight months after Penny came to live with us, our oldest son became engaged. John and Rita had dated for more than two years, and we knew her well. It was January, and we were bursting with excitement and plans for their late summer wedding.

Though Rita worked Monday through Friday, she always made time to visit awhile with Penny on the weekend. Penny adored her four grandchildren, and Bob and I thought she might enjoy a special time when the bride-and-groom-to-be could share their wonderful news with her. It would be a cozy chat, a time for all of us to think back and look ahead together. Two generations, Penny's and ours, would welcome Rita into our family. I could hardly wait for the day to arrive.

At last the chosen Saturday came. Penny waited in the reclining chair, wearing a pale blue shawl which complimented her brushed hair and trace of cheek color. When the four of us walked into her room, Bob grinned, facing his mother so she wouldn't miss a word.

"Mom, we have some big news!"

"My goodness, what's happening?"

"I think I'll let John tell . . . ."

John gave his grandmother a big hug. "Grandmere, you've visited lots of times with Rita . . . ."

"Oh, yes! I know Rita." Penny nodded, years of instinctive social skills guiding her like a genetic radar.

"Well, Grandmere, Rita and I are engaged! We're going to be married in September!"

We could tell Penny was pleased. As Bob and I pulled up chairs, John and Rita described exactly how he had proposed. Rita patted Penny's hand as they talked. "When I get my ring, I'll show it to you, Grandmere," she promised.

"That'll be nice." Then suddenly Penny looked directly at me, her empty smile mirroring the one we had first seen the evening we arrived in Phoenix.

"Mary? Who is this I'm talking to?" Irritation colored her words.

That's when I learned that stress triggers hot flashes. I felt my face turn scarlet and looked longingly at the tightly closed window. I wanted to dive through it into a deep snowbank—glass, screen, and all. Instead I managed an awkward laugh and glanced at Rita. She smiled back. I could tell she was uneasy, but understood.

Bob and John came to the rescue with small talk, jokes, and a graceful end to the conversation. As we walked down the hall I was certain I would someday laugh about this incident. But right then I was mortified.

Penny, of course, couldn't help her nonexistent memory. But I felt foolish for allowing something like this to happen. I had pushed ahead, living in an imagined world of generational sharing. I had wanted all of us together, including Penny, to welcome Rita into our family. Instead, Rita ended up embarrassed, Penny confused, and I ready to burst into flame at any moment.

That day Bob and I joined the thousands of others in the so-called sandwich generation. On one side of us were John and Rita. On the other was Penny. We were the filling.

Our grandparents probably felt similar pressure at times, but it wasn't the same. Then, as now, nearly three-fourths of all caregivers were women—wives, daughters, or daughters-in-law of the person needing care. But people then didn't live into their mid-eighties and beyond as they do today. Children didn't defer marriage into the late twenties and early thirties to go to school or develop careers. And adult children, like us, weren't caught in the middle. Our twentieth century has built a real triple-decker.

Sandwich-generation women experience pressure from every side. Children may still be at home. If not, they are conducting job searches, planning to marry, or launching careers. Either way, they want and need to talk things over with their mother. She wants and needs to talk to them.

If she is married, her husband may want her taking part in functions relevant to his peaking career. Or perhaps he has recently retired, a major life change for him (not to mention his wife). They may have saved for years to go on a gala postretirement trip. Their children grown, the two of them look forward to a heady springtime of new freedoms.

Many mid-life women work outside the home, relishing the stimulation and challenge. Often in their most productive work years, they enjoy pouring their considerable talents, training, and energy into a career.

The average sandwich-generation woman is 57 years old. This means that on top of everything else, half of them are entering or in the midst of menopause, with all of its singular joys. This can be a time of exhilarating self-discovery, renewed sexuality, and overall well-being. Thirty or more productive years usually lie ahead.

But menopause can also be a time of loss: of changing appearance, decreased energy, and children who are no longer dependent. The journey through menopause is usually not difficult. But it will go most smoothly for the woman gifted with time to chart the course ahead, and with time for herself. Sandwich-generation women have neither.

As John and Rita's wedding date approached, we learned what a sandwich filling feels like. Because we have a backyard full of roses and pine trees, Bob and I offered to have their rehearsal dinner and reception in our home. It was a busy, wonderful time. But the closer the big day came, the more convinced we were that somebody should stay with Penny the entire time. Someone besides us. Debbi, one of the nurse's aides who helped Penny mornings and evenings, agreed to provide that care.

At last the wedding day arrived, sparkling with sunshine. We arranged chairs on the back lawn, opened and hung pink paper bells from wide ribbons, and covered tables in the garage with sheets to hold extra food. Being able to forget about Penny's well-being proved to be one of the wisest decisions we had ever made.

Debbi arrived early, carrying a supply of rollers to curl and wave Penny's hair. After the family left for the church, Debbi gave her a bath, worked the rollers into place, and started the long process of getting her dressed.

To Penny, dressing didn't mean slipping into a muumuu. It meant hose, heels, and a tailored navy dress with a lapel pin. Above all, it meant a girdle. Debbi told us how that went hours later, when the house was adrift in boxed presents, birdseed, and wilting pink roses. She had managed to work the girdle partway over Penny's ample hips when it started to rip.

"This tore a little bit, I'm afraid."

"We can just use pins," Penny encouraged her. "But I need to rest." Debbi eased her into the recliner.

I have no idea how old the girdle was when Azava poured Penny into it before her flight from Phoenix. Conservative archaeological estimates would put its age at about twenty-five years.

Five minutes later Debbi helped Penny to her feet, tugged a little more, and felt it rip again. "Do you think we could do without this, Penny?" After all, the navy dress had a wide pleated skirt, and the hose could be secured with something. Twine, maybe. Or yarn. Anything.

Penny's blue eyes narrowed. "It'll go on. Keep trying. Now I want to rest awhile."

Five or ten minutes later Debbi braced Penny's arms on the bed and pulled again. This time two hidden pins snapped open, scratching Debbi's wrist. Penny announced she needed to rest some more.

Finally, challenged anew, Debbi braced one knee against the bed and gave a herculean tug. The sagging, ancient elastic settled comfortably around Penny's waist. Debbi partially closed the gaping hole in the yellowed front panel with industrial-weight safety pins. Perspiring, she patted Penny's hand. "There! We made it. Does that feel all right?"

"Wonderful!"

From that point on it was clear sailing. With Debbi propelling the wheelchair, Penny enjoyed every minute of the reception. Pictures of her wearing a pink and silver corsage while relishing a crab-stuffed pastry testify to the fun she had. Her girdle was in place. Let the music begin.

The scratches on Debbi's hands and wrists healed up in about a week. Penny went to bed earlier than usual that night, thrilled with the first of her grandchildren's weddings. For two whole days she remembered and talked about it. And Bob and I danced together in the violet shadows of early evening, watching the bride's sheer veil ripple behind her. For that one timeless day, both sides of the sandwich rested lightly on the filling. And I didn't have a single hot flash.

Having somebody else care for Penny all day long had been glorious, but hardly practical. I gathered up tablecloths, tossed out wilted flowers, and froze the wedding cake top, all the while assessing my role as a sandwich filling. There had to be a way to sift and sort the fast returning pressures. I thought wistfully of the simple priorities that used to keep my life in balance—before I became a primary caregiver.

God's Ideal

I had always believed that priorities were like grains of sand in an hourglass. The whole thing was important, but I needed a clear vision of what stayed on top. Like a watercolor painting, the edge of one priority continually blended into another. Sorting them out helped me orient my life according to God's plan instead of responding to the person who complained or yelled the loudest.

My most important priority had always been my relationship with God. I needed to carve out time with Him every day to read the Bible, pray, and bathe myself in worship—alone and with my church family. Nothing I did felt quite right until I first spent time with the loving God who created and sustained me.

My second priority, believe it or not, was myself. I knew if I were to have anything to give away to others, I had to allow myself to become the person God intended when He designed me. Time spent developing and caring for myself wasn't narcissism. It was a living thank-you to my heavenly Father.

Because I was married, my third priority was Bob. Scripture instructs husbands and wives to love, respect, praise, honor, and care for each other. Why? Because it honors God. The most powerful testimony a husband and wife will ever give the world is the quality of their marriage and family.

My children were my fourth priority. Whether molding clay dinosaurs as toddlers or teaching school as adults, they were my children. At every age they needed my unconditional love, my prayers, my encouragement. And whether first grader or chairman of the board, each one needed me to let go and allow God to do His work in their lives.

My fifth priority was my home, whether I had an outside job or not. Our home became my family's daily springboard into the world, undergirding all of us for whatever the day might bring.

Involvement beyond the home was my last priority. When everything else was in order, I didn't have much time for that one—especially when I worked away from home eight hours a day. I needed to prayerfully evaluate how I used my extra time and energy.

Enter Caregiving

God's ideal priorities weren't hard for me to understand. They made sense. They had always worked. But when I became a caregiver my priorities became distorted, like objects reflected in a fun-house mirror. Caregiving dwarfed my top priorities. It inflated lesser ones into misshapen giants. And it blasted my second priority, myself, clear out of the water.

"The hardest part," wrote a caregiver whose husband has Alzheimer's disease, "was accepting the fact that my life was going down the tube, and feeling the frustration that I couldn't do a thing about the situation. It limits every area of my life. I can't even go to the neighbor's for coffee without being sure that my husband has been to the bathroom first."

I don't know about you, but carving out time for prayer and Bible study has never slipped smoothly into my schedule. It's rarely convenient. I struggle daily to make time alone with my Lord the highest priority of my life.

When I began caring for Penny, I knew God was with me moment by moment. But finding time to be alone with Him was like scaling a spiritual Mount Everest. Time to sit down? No, I'd fall asleep. Time to read Scripture? No, I needed to dig out my old nursing notes on bedsore prevention. It was months before I could weave quiet time with the Lord into my day, usually in the early afternoon while Penny dozed.

A husband-and-wife caregiving team will have miniscule amounts of energy to devote to one another. "In later years it was necessary to have someone with my mother at all times," wrote Barbara Chinn, a caregiver for fourteen years. "My husband and I went out together very seldom."

"The hardest part," added another, "was sharing my home and my wife."

"It was a complete commitment, and time away was difficult," shared the wife who helped her husband care for both his parents. "We took turns getting away. It sure made the times we could go together very precious."

Besides worrying about their relative, spouse caregiving teams also worry about each other. It's painful to watch fatigue lines and dark circles appear in your beloved's face, yet be helpless to make things easier.

"The hardest part of caregiving for me," remembers Dean Price, "was the mental strain on my wife. After all, this was her mother. But the experience brought us closer together and also strengthened our faith in the Lord. We needed that support."

Joint caregiving often brings conflict over little things, leaving one or the other spouse caught in the middle. "We had some hard feelings toward each other," Don Bogart remembers. "Mother was a bit of a manipulator, which caused a little problem."

A wife with hot flashes may want the temperature of her house on the cool side. Her husband understands. But how do they respond to her ninety-three-year-old-father, hunched on the couch wearing ski socks, mittens, long underwear, a wool beanie, and covered with stadium blankets?

As mentioned earlier, sexuality may be another major area of loss for a caregiving husband and wife. "I think jointly caring for an in-law could possibly affect a couple's relationship," wrote Donna Ring. "If you're too tired for love-making, and it could certainly happen, it could build resentment."

Both husband and wife long for the comfort and release God provides through their physical relationship. Yet exhaustion usually wins out. When caregiving ends, intimacy almost always returns—richer and more beautiful than before. Yet most couples will still need to work hard to renew their relationship after caregiving's all-consuming demands.

"We don't have much to talk about anymore," shared a caregiver after the death of her mother-in-law. "Apparently everything surrounding Mom had filled our dinner conversations. There is much silence now. I hope that we find new things to discuss soon."

A caregiving season may distort extended family relationships as well. Old problems don't get any better, and new ones continually surface. "Mediating between Mother and my sister was the hardest part," shared Bob Pettit. "They rarely had seen eye to eye, and that didn't change as Mother continued to get worse."

Donajeanne Bogart wrote that "the most frustrating thing was when relatives came to visit. I never knew what was expected of me. Were they there primarily to visit Mom, or us? How visible should we be? When mutual friends came, what should we do?"

We have already talked about the extent to which caregiving distorts a single person's life. Unless she finds some help, carrying the full load by herself may devastate social and other interests. The single caregiver also faces the danger of developing a morbid preoccupation with her loved one's condition. As other parts of her single life slip away, her task may take on grotesque proportions. This can lead to severe depression when her caregiving season ends.

Children living in a caregiving home will inevitably be affected by what they see, hear, and experience. Older children, though concerned about grandparents or other relatives, worry most about their own parents. "They were glad Grandpa didn't have to go to a nursing home," wrote Carolyn Bradley of her four children. "But they also felt protective toward us, that we wouldn't be overburdened."

Younger children should be encouraged to take an active part in the experience. "Let kids interact and provide gestures of love," urges Jane Hutchinson. "Don't protect them from the patient or the feelings you are dealing with. Talk with them. Reassure them of your love for one another (wife and husband), and of the security of a *commitment* that sticks it out."

Caregivers who experience the severest sandwich-generation pressures are those who also have a chronically ill or diminished capacity child. "With the exception of Dianne," shared Donajeanne about her mentally deficient fourth child, "they all seemed happy with having 'Grammy'

123

in her apartment upstairs. Dianne resented her at times. I can still hear her expounding, 'No—Gamma!' and then adding, 'Baby!' She wanted all my time herself."

The caregiver who also juggles an outside job endures relentless tension. For some, the job is a place of refuge. "I never could have managed without my job," wrote one caregiver. "All day at home would have been too much."

But though invigorated by her work, the caregiver can rarely devote herself entirely to its demands. She usually fields several care-related phone interruptions each day. She is frequently worried, preoccupied with problems at home, short of sleep, and late to work.

Increasing numbers of employers are becoming sensitive to this double bind. A few pioneers are moving into uncharted territory by arranging elder-care centers for their employees. Mothers relax and produce better quality work when their small children are well cared for. The same holds true for sandwich-generation people.

Taking the Squeeze Out of the Sandwich

Until a caregiving season ends and/or the children move on, many sandwich-generation people will live with that delicatessen feeling. Whether you are peanut butter, cream cheese, or pastrami, from time to time you'll feel as if an elephant sat on you. Squished. And your once well-ordered priorities will get placed on permanent hold.

But we can distance ourselves from the deli through thought, planning, and determination. The key is balance. We need to search for equilibrium as we tiptoe through the mine field of Grandma's midnight stroll next door, toddlers with diarrhea, and scalding hot flashes.

On the one hand we obey Christ's call to servanthood. We don't demand everything our way. We know life isn't a cast of characters named Me, Myself, and I. We are willing to sacrifice much of our lives for those we love and honor. Yet there is a danger here, especially for Christians.

I've always had trouble cheering for those ancient saints who deserted home, husband, and children so they could live as hermits and pursue God. We must question any ministry, however admirable, that cuts family bonds. Under that kind of pseudonoble pressure, the whole sandwich soon disintegrates.

We need to weigh our God-given priorities alongside the biblical call to self-sacrifice. We've examined our ideal priorities. We've seen what caregiving can do to them. But even when they get distorted, God's pattern doesn't change. My personal relationship with God, my marriage, and my children remain my top priorities. I must fit my parents in around the edges. If I totally sacrifice myself for one or the other, I'll have nothing left for either.

Abandoning family in the name of caregiving does not honor God. Nor does dodging my loved one's needs in the name of ideal priorities. I must guard against going all one direction or the other. I must pray daily for balance, wisdom, insight, realism, and common sense as I work my way through the maze of multigenerational caregiving.

Whether you're a married or single caregiver, that squished sandwich feeling diminishes when you talk to someone—regularly. Far too many caregivers skirt this primordial survival skill, mumbling that, "I never talk to anyone! There's no time! Besides, I'm too tired!"

Talk-time won't arrive by Federal Express, tied up with red, white, and blue ribbons. It will only happen only when you make it happen. If you and your spouse share caregiving, schedule definite times together each and every week. Write them on your main calendar, in big letters. When those times come, claw your way to the front door. Go to a coffee shop. Have an English muffin. Have lunch. Have a hot fudge sundae. Somehow, get away—together.

"You need frequent breathers," urges a caregiver, "more time away, if only a few hours for a movie—or just lunch."

When the two of you sit down, ask how the other is doing. How are you doing as a couple? Review the week: what went wrong, what went right, and your feelings about both. If one of you is deeply discouraged and perhaps questioning continued caregiving, take a good look at your situation. Your job is difficult enough when both of you pull together. Without that unity, it's impossible.

"We cared for my mother for fourteen years," remembers Barbara Chinn. "Toward the end it became very difficult, but now it is much more difficult having her in the convalescent hospital. She has been there one month. I think getting out with my husband and spending some time alone each week is the most helpful thing."

Another woman, who with her husband cared eight years for her mother, said that, "My husband loved my mother and was most cooperative. I respected him for this. I needed his support. I don't see how anyone could do it if one partner objected."

"Home care is not for everyone," suggests Kaye Kepple. "If your spouse is opposed to the idea, I would look at other options. But caring for my mom helped my friends and others feel comfortable and learn to minister to people like her. They started out by feeling extremely awkward, but soon would be giving Mom hugs, holding her hand, feeding her, and even wiping the drool off her chin."

If you or your spouse think you're possibly burning out as caregivers, consider placing your relative in a short-term nursing facility. A week or two (or three) of rest and freedom from tension often galvanizes caregivers and enables them to pick up the load again. Many military families are assigned vacations with a wonderful title: "R and R." It's short for rest and relaxation. If your circumstances allow it, arrange for your loved one to visit a good short-term care center every six months or so while you take a richly deserved caregiving R and R.

During talk-times with your spouse, regularly consider other options. Can you bring someone in to help for an extra day, or hour, each week? Should you take a more serious look at sharing care with other family members? If they don't volunteer, take the initiative. Insist on working something out that will reduce the pressure on you.

Be sure to also review your many caregiving chores. Are they fairly divided between the two of you, and whoever else lives in your home? Talk about what you do in terms of time spent on specific jobs. How many hours a day does each of you have for caregiving tasks? How much are you giving? Talk also about energy output: Is the total fairly divided?

Last of all, take time to pray together. If you're comfortable with it, pray right there in the coffee shop. Or wait until later. Weekly prayer coming from a searching, surrendered heart energizes caregiving as nothing else can.

The single person has an even deeper need to talk and unload. Spending time weekly with a support group or an encouraging, caring friend is essential. Yet because she is her loved one's mainstay, she may be far more reluctant to leave. "When my husband was in a nursing facility for six weeks," shared a wife whose husband has senile dementia, "I actually made myself ill by spending eight to ten hours a day with him. I don't think I could do that again."

It can't be stressed too much: the single or spouse caregiver must force herself to get away regularly. She must build a solid, reliable outside support system. To neglect this is to invite disaster as the demands of caregiving grow.

The first section of your caregiving notebook will also help you back away from your feelings of pressure. As time allows, make journal entries about specific problems in your caregiving situation. Does Mom refuse to come out of her room when your daughter's best friend visits? Does she refuse to leave her room no matter who visits? Did Dad accuse you of stealing from him last week? Has your invalid husband taken to calling you by a new name—the one your mother used when you were in trouble?

Be honest and specific about every area that bothers you, then prayerfully assess them one by one. Can the situation be improved? Is it time to confront? (If so, read the next chapter first.) Have you failed to relinquish an area you cannot change? Write, assess, and pray.

At any stage of life, it's important to do something just for you. During mid-life, this outlet holds the sandwich together. "I know I need something for myself," wrote

Barbara Eagan after seven years of secondary caregiving. "I think after Christmas I will look into returning to college again. A year ago I started taking jazz and tap classes. I feel very good about that. After sitting forty hours a week at a desk for so many years, I really like being more active physically."

You may need to get tough to create time for yourself, especially if you're a primary caregiver. Remember that your loved one is likely to want you, and you alone, to care for his needs. But make up your mind to do something meaningful to you: knitting lessons, golf, Bible study, aerobics, calligraphy, auto repair, or whatever. Nobody else has to like it. This activity is *yours*.

After you choose something, give yourself permission to do it. Then insist on doing it weekly, or as often as you can swing it. Arrange for whatever your relative needs while you're gone. Then get started! You'll enjoy every minute of it. And in the process you'll set some small limits on your caregiving involvement that will be healthy for everyone.

One final strategy for sandwich-generation survival: laugh every chance you get. The Book of Proverbs offers some wonderful advice: "A joyful heart is good medicine, but a broken spirit dries up the bones" (Proverbs 17:22). Mid-life brings enough dry bone problems. So laugh when your face turns scarlet and it's snowing outside. Laugh when you feel like a sandwich flattened by an elephant. No matter what your circumstances, somehow, some way, laugh!

"Father, I feel as if I'm suffocating. I feel so much pressure . . . ."

"Lift up your eyes, My treasured one. I am bearing your burden."

"Even in this, Lord?"

"Even in this."

Chapter Eight
Tyrants and Tears

Ted Hutchinson, a pastor and caregiver, expresses an all-too-common problem for those who provide home care. "Mom argues and gets angry a lot," he says. "She gets frustrated at us for 'going behind her back,' withholding mail, or writing in her checkbook. We try to explain to her, yet she can't remember for two minutes (literally) the explanation. We go over and over it till finally I just get up and leave. Explanations and answers do no good at all."

"It is hard to know when and how to take more control," he continues, "such as taking over her checkbook, selling her car, renting or selling her home, getting her to take her medicine, bathe, keep doctor's appointments, and so forth. When do we 'go behind her back' to do what we believe must be done, even though it may be against her will and even her convictions? Do we just do it and ignore the tirade?"

After the death of Ted's father, his mother, Janet, had gotten along well for eight years. Then, like a rose at summer's end, her memory faded. She forgot appointments and dates with friends, and rarely left her small home. One day she fell, requiring surgical repair of her left leg. When she could leave the hospital, Ted and his wife Jane invited her to recuperate with them and their three small children.

But Janet soon begged to go home, despite "Welcome Gramma" banners on the wall, get-well cards in her entry-level bedroom and bath, spontaneous playtimes with grandchildren, and faithful visits from her pastor and friends.

"Mom has never done crafts," Jane reported, "yet she often complains of being bored. She reads a lot, but often it's the same thing over and over." Janet had no idea she wasn't able to drive, remember where she was, bathe herself, shop for groceries, cook, or keep track of medications from one hour to the next.

"The children," Ted said, "are asking more and more questions about why Gramma acts angry or confused, or doesn't 'like' them." Jane added that, "I've had to let go of what I'd *like* her to be as a grandma."

Janet had only Medicare, as for years she had resisted buying supplemental health insurance. Her injury required physical therapy, a custom-made leg brace, and high-top athletic shoes. The mounting bills forced Ted and Jane to consider using Janet's pension check to meet expenses. But when they attempted to include her in the financial planning for this, tempers flared.

With each discussion Janet became more frustrated, confused, stubborn, and angry. Each time she ended up in tears. Jane wrote, "Her accusations and attitude toward my husband (her only son), especially related to money, were impossible not to take personally."

The Hutchinson family had reached one of caregiving's universal flash points: finances. Other potentially explosive parts of any caregiving relationship include conflicts over medication, equipment, dietary restrictions, physical limitations, and the plans of other family members.

On the surface, the conflict might seem like Round One of "Tyrant Janet vs. Longsuffering Ted and Jane." But at the core of the family's volcanic flash fire smoldered a struggle for control. Janet was desperate to regain command of her life. After all, she had directed it very well for most of her seventy-plus years. Ted and Jane's well-intentioned agenda formed a concrete wall Janet could not get over or around.

Sometimes, especially if mental impairment is part of the diagnosis, your loved one's control-loss anxiety may reveal itself through physical symptoms. Be alert to signals such as an excessive need to sleep, colitis, irritability, shortness of breath, constant complaining, impotence, insomnia, and allergic flare-ups. Any of these may signal a relative's unexpressed apprehension.

When we found Penny molding a bowel movement in her hands the day we were to fly to Washington, her action was a message to us, not a deliberate attempt to make us miss the plane. At the deepest level of her being, she was calling out for help. The drapes were being drawn on her beloved home of over fifty years, and there was nothing she could do to stop it. She had lost control, and she knew it. Penny's infantile behavior, caused by her stroke-damaged brain, reflected her profound anxiety and helplessness.

People who have physical limitations but intact mental faculties frequently focus their struggle for control on the caregiver. Their weapons are tears and hurtful words, aimed at the closest target—you. Nothing you do is adequate. Nothing you do measures up.

"The struggle for control is most decidedly our problem," states Maurine Kalk, an across-town caregiver for her 79-year-old mother-in-law. "Her control-loss anxiety is at times profound. It expresses itself in constant complaining. She feels no matter how much I do for her, it isn't enough."

Yet when friends and neighbors drop by with cookies, Maurine's relative (and probably yours) smiles and inquires about the person's family. It's clear that your visitors think you're exaggerating. Nobody believes that this delightful woman cracking jokes expects instant room service and a hot lunch of her choice seven days a week. Or that she frequently describes, making sure you hear every word, other homes where "they treated me like a queen." Your loved one's public and private faces are often drastically different.

Some dependent relatives bend over backwards to make each day pleasant. Others are impossible to please, seizing every opportunity to criticize and demand more. Such ongoing battles, if unchecked, will damage even the most dedicated family circle. Symptomatic flash fires, whatever the fuel, are soon forgotten. But the smoldering root cause, your loved one's fierce fight for independence, will continue to singe the edges of your caregiving relationship.

A single caregiver who has no one else for relief or emotional support may be overcome by a relative's endless objections and arguing. Soon she, like thousands of others, invents ways to avoid her loved one.

The burden is equally difficult for a married caregiver. "I felt confident in the physical handling," reported the wife whose husband's right side was paralyzed by a stroke. "But I also felt trapped, grieving for his loss. I felt depressed and panicky. I had to make all the decisions, complicated by his constant mind changing of what he wished to do. He demanded immediate compliance with his needs or desires." She found that the hardest part of caregiving was contending with her husband's depression and irritability.

It's not hard to understand his feelings, and in small ways to identify with his anxiety. But his attempts to regain control of his life make taking care of him increasingly stressful.

"How did you sleep last night?"

"I didn't sleep at all." His eyes look down, his pale face turns away.

"Not at all?"

"You heard me."

He isn't angry at you, and he probably slept better than he admits. He is furious about his situation and fights back with the only weapon left—control of *something*, even if it is only the last word about how he slept. But before long, he becomes a tyrant.

Your relative has another powerful weapon you have probably discovered by now—guilt.

"Dear, I'm going to the store now. I won't be long."

"Do you have to go?"

"We need groceries," you explain.

"You never sit down with me anymore. All you do is work!"

The unspoken message is that your loved one is lonely, and you're the cause. You can tell he's thinking: *Don't go to the store. In fact, don't go anywhere. Just stay here, talk to me, be my world, and make my life the way it used to be.* Your relative shifts a burden of guilt onto you, and it is heavy as lead.

If this situation goes unchecked, he wins. He assumes a warped control, with the family bending and scraping to avoid his outbursts. They tiptoe around his easy chair. They soon discover ways to get from one end of the house to the other without passing his room.

Such tyranny in a family cannot honor God, who equally loves both halves of the caregiving equation. When the Pharisees asked Jesus which was the great commandment in the law, He answered, "'You shall love the Lord your God with all your heart, and with all your soul, and with all your mind.' This is the great and foremost commandment. The second is like it, 'You shall love your neighbor as yourself.' On these two commandments depend the whole Law and the Prophets" (Matthew 22:37-40).

Jesus' statement cannot be interpreted to suggest that we should indulge a relative's every whim and neglect our own needs. That approach may work during the first altruistic months of giving care, but it can't last. Not only is it unrealistic, it is unhealthy for all concerned.

Jesus commands all of us to love ourselves. Self-love then becomes a model for loving others. Without question, we need to empathize with our relative's losses and desire for independence. In many practical ways we need to give him ongoing alternatives, allowing him to do everything he can for himself. But if he chooses to use guilt, anger, accusations, or tears to manipulate the caregiver, she needs to lovingly correct him—whatever his condition.

As a caregiver, you have at your command three interventions as you care for a manipulative loved one. All are appropriate courses of action based on Christ's commandment that we are to love our neighbors as we love ourselves. Regular, periodic use of each is essential to successful caregiving. The first intervention takes place as you pray. The second and third take place with your relative.

Prayerful Identification

The foundation of your caregiving is frequent, prayerful identification with your loved one. This is best done during your daily prayer time. Imagine taking tight hold of Jesus' outstretched hand, and ask Him to help you step into your relative's shoes. Allow the Holy Spirit to lead you to a deeper, more intimate understanding of this person you are caring for, whether child, parent, grandparent, or spouse.

Imagine yourself forced to leave your own home— required to rent or even sell it. Perhaps you remember only that it is gone, but can't remember why. Imagine being compelled by circumstances to sell or give away your lamps, china, glasses, trip souvenirs, flower vases, stamp collection, sewing machine, tools, canning jars, glasses, high school yearbooks, the children's old basketball trophies, linens, and your great-aunt's Dresden coffeepot.

Though you increasingly loathe change, you must watch the sure things of your life fade away one by one. You must choose four pictures out of your twenty, to be hung on walls you have never seen. You must decide which pots and pans to keep and give away. You wonder secretly whether you'll ever again wear the red, white, and blue dress you sewed for the family reunion thirty years ago.

You feel yourself moved into one of your own adult children's homes, feel yourself squeezed into the middle of lives already too busy. You sense the family waiting to hear you rave about the room they've prepared for you, a room you can't stand.

What happened to the neighbor's kitten who used to come in the afternoon, whose skinny hind legs were too big for its body? Who will water the lilac bushes that grew against the back fence? And who will make potato salad for the annual block party?

Imagine yourself still able to walk, studying yourself in front of a mirror and wondering if the reflection is really you. When did you get so old? Where did your ambition go? Where are all your friends, and the money you worked so long to save?

"I never wanted to be a burden," you whisper to the person in the mirror, desperate for reassurance that you aren't. But in the epicenter of your being, you sense that no matter what they tell you, you are a heavy and cumbersome burden to the ones you love the most.

Keep allowing the Lord to direct your imagination and memory. Allow Jesus to help you focus on everything you know about the *person*, rather than the relative, you are caring for. Think through the following paragraph, as if you were your loved one:

"My name is _____ and my occupation used to be _____ . I enjoy many things in life, especially _____ . The most important thing of all to me is _____ . I have always loved doing _____ . But I was afraid of _____ . Today I am a little afraid, too, especially of _____ . Sometimes I feel like _____ ."

For example, exactly who is Ted's mother, Janet, whose ongoing senile dementia keeps her shuffling through a box of ten-year-old receipts each day? It's easy to forget that she is a college graduate and was a locally renowned Bible teacher who formed the other half of her husband Normand's nearly half-century Seattle area pastorate.

A powerful ministerial team, Normand and Janet played a major role in establishing Pacific Northwest Christian camping. For years Janet taught Old Testament theology, Christian Education, and English to both high school and college students. Seattle newspapers published her articles for the religion section. The room she lives in at her son's home reflects her gift for organization and order. Now Normand's sudden death, her osteoporosis, and her progressive senile dementia have left Janet depressed and suspicious of those closest to her.

Prayerful identification, using everything you can learn about your loved one, allows the Holy Spirit to bring his or her almost forgotten past into your present. In a sense, your relative is behind bars: the bars of inability. But you can peek between them and discover who's inside. Prayerful identification, repeated at convenient intervals, will defuse your anger. It will help you say, "I understand," and mean it.

Loving Confrontation

Your second caregiving intervention is loving confrontation, with strong emphasis on the word *loving*. Such confrontation refuses to accept the burdens your relative would shift onto you. Aging and illness aren't easy, and nobody welcomes either. But they are facts of this life. Your well of sympathy can be drained only so much. Long before it runs dry, you may be able to help your loved one assume some of the present reality—even if it has to be repeated hours later. But loving confrontation must be done with exquisite gentleness, as would Jesus Himself.

"I've come to the point where I don't feel that I *have* to make things work out right," Ted observed. "If Mom understands and accepts, great. If she doesn't, I still do what I believe is right and best, and take the lumps. As a result I'm beginning to worry less, argue less, and explain less. I'm trying to see to it that Mom has the best care. I'm not trying to make her happy, though it would be grand to learn to do and say things in a way that entertain her and brighten her day. When I cannot make Mom happy, I have to realize she's unhappy because she can't remember reasons and causes. The present is distorted and her future is filled with uncertainty. Breaks in simple routines are monumental disasters."

One caregiver's mother, who has had limited vision for many years, lives in a retirement complex thirty minutes away. Not long ago her daughter, who owns a growing small business and had been unable to visit for a week, phoned to ask how she was.

"There's a big pile of mail I need to read." Her mother sounded on the verge of tears.

"Maybe one of your neighbors could read it to you."

"Oh, I'm waiting for you." Her voice quavered. "But you haven't been out to see me in days."

It's nice to be needed, but there's a painful subliminal message here: "I thought you loved me, but now I'm not so sure." This partially blind mother walks around her apartment, uses the phone, and takes care of her personal needs. She is of sound mind, with overall good health. Only her vision limits her, but, probably not deliberately, she is milking that for all it's worth.

We wouldn't tolerate such behavior in children. We would remind them of all they can do, encourage them to try new things, and help them perceive the handicap as a challenge for excellence. But many people allow an ill or impaired older relative to get away with murder. Without purposeful intervention, the corpse may be the caregiver's.

The alternative is loving confrontation, which includes letting your relative know you have limits. You cannot be in all places at all times. Any loved one who tries to force you to do that—consciously or unconsciously—needs loving correction.

"Mom, because I work in the shop, I can't get out to see you as often as I'd like to. You need to find somebody close by to help with your mail."

"Oh, I don't want to bother anybody."

"Mom, you're bothering me, and that really isn't fair. I'll come out just as soon as I can. But meanwhile, you need somebody to help you."

"I don't know anybody."

"Call the church. Tell them you need someone to help you out a few hours a week."

"That's so embarrassing. I feel like an old lady."

"I'm sorry, Mom. but until I can get over there, you

need to make other arrangements to get the mail read. Could I call the church for you?"

During this conversation your heart will beat faster than normal, your palms will perspire, you will feel guilty and downright mean. Mom will argue, sulk, and be unhappy.

Confrontation, even when lovingly done, is uncomfortable for everyone involved. It takes practice. And thankfully, it won't be needed for every crisis. If you are part of a caregiving couple, you may find that one of you confronts more easily than the other.

"My problem is that her attitude makes me want to withdraw and let Gail do what is necessary," explained Maurine. "Mary likes to win—to have us revolving around her plans. I cannot correct her yet . . . she would get very angry with me. Gail does better at calling her hand than I do."

This arrangement is not uncommon among caregiving couples, and is a good temporary solution. But as time goes on, it is wise to work toward consistent, gentle confrontation from both.

When you first make a stand on an issue, you may not notice an immediate change in your loved one. But in the days that follow, you will almost certainly experience its impact. As certain problems are dumped back where they belong, your relative will be forced to assume control of at least some areas of his or her life—and leave others to you.

"Nobody but you knows what I want done with my bills."

"I'll get to them soon, Dad."

"These can't wait! Oh, I feel so helpless these days . . . ."

"Dad, I can't right now. I'll get the bills paid. But I'm not going to do them this minute. Let's put them in a stack right here, and I'll get to them as soon as it's convenient."

Dad won't like that reply one bit. But as you take steps to protect your own time and space, you are also taking steps to ensure that the caregiving relationship continues. If your loved one lives with you, loving confrontation is a must.

The Tough Love Talk

Your final caregiving intervention is a tough love talk, again underscoring the word *love*. It is best undertaken in private, with the television, radio, or stereo turned off. Try to sit beside your relative or at an angle, not directly facing him. Somehow, manage a smile. Keep in mind that many people maintain control by walking away whenever they sense trouble. You can get around that problem by planning to conduct your tough love talk in the car, with a third person driving.

After Penny had been with us a little over a year, she one day refused to take her vitamin, pain, and heart pills. "You want 'em?" she asked me after several tries. "Here!" With a steady hand she tossed them all over the room.

I spent about ten minutes on my hands and knees, searching through the carpet for tiny pills hidden behind table legs and under the bed. When I finally offered her the pills again (ignoring the germ theory), she clapped both hands over her mouth.

I gave up and walked around outside until my homicidal instincts wore off. Then I returned to her room, turned off the television, sat near her recliner, and tried to smile. I acknowledged how much things had changed for her. I told her I knew it was hard for all of us at times. I encouraged her that things would get better, but we both had to work to make that happen.

I tried to keep smiling, and said how happy we were to have her with us. I explained that for our family routine to work, I had to get out for a little while each day to shop and run errands. I didn't tell her that without some time away, I felt like a caged lion.

And then I got lovingly tough. I told Penny that for her to be here, certain things had to happen. The first was that she had to help me. She could not throw her pills on the floor. (Though after I evaluated the situation, I began to crush her pills and mix them with yogurt.) At that point, Penny looked away and tried several times to change the subject.

139

Second, I said that her wants and needs were very important to us, but that Bob and I had needs, too. Everything in the house could not revolve around her. Again, she tried to change the subject. I ignored her. Firmly, I told her how fortunate she was to be in our home, not somewhere else. I meant every word of it. I explained that our arrangement worked because all of us helped each other.

Most dependent people, with the exception of those with Alzheimer's disease or advanced dementias, can be helped to assume some responsibility for their words and actions. The elderly and chronically ill, whatever their ages, frequently have tantrums, walk away, sulk, cry, and refuse to speak. They do this for one reason: they want their own way. One woman, bedridden, wet the bed whenever her husband took one of his weekly half days off.

"Mom's back there complaining because her dinner's late."

"Dad's sulking because I'm going to a movie."

"Harry says I'm exactly like his Aunt Sue who spent half her life in a mental institution."

And on and on. Far too many caregivers accept this kind of manipulative abuse. Most people able to live with their family know very well when they're being unreasonable. Too many caregivers dash through the grocery store, squeeze in a trip to the surgical supply house, then abandon the precious half hour they'd saved for coffee and a muffin while they race back to their loved one. Unless your relative is dying, perhaps it's time for a tough love talk.

My conversation with Penny lasted twenty minutes. I repeated the key points about five times each. That we were very glad she was in our home. (I meant that, too.) That I had to be able to get out each day. That her part in all of it was to make things as easy as possible for the family. And that I loved her too much to allow her to throw her pills on the floor.

Did she sit there and apologize? No. She stared at me with too-bright eyes, smiling slightly. But she knew I meant it. Having her with us, even under ideal conditions, was exhausting. Without her cooperation, it was impossible. I don't know if my speech registered or not. I do know that from that day on, she was far more cooperative. And she never threw anything on the floor again.

That tough love talk wasn't easy for me. As with loving confrontation, my heart pounded and I wanted it to end. My daughter-in-law's sense of hospitality and good manners flew in the face of what had to be said. But even more than I wanted it over, I wanted Penny to continue living with us. And I knew myself well enough to realize I couldn't allow her to trap me with anger and tears, intentional or not.

Again and again, Jesus forced His disciples and those around Him to make choices, to take responsibility for what they did. Unless they're in a coma, our relatives can do the same. Infirmity and age cannot be allowed to rob caregivers of self-esteem and energy.

Never forget that without you, your loved one would be someplace else: perhaps with another relative, or in a care facility with a roommate who cries all night, or sleeping on a sidewalk heater grate. You are your loved one's lifeline. That lifeline deserves meticulous care, regular maintenance, and periodic checkups.

"Lord, I feel like a figure in an antique paper-weight. An invisible hand is shaking up my life, blurring all the familiar landmarks. . . ."

"There is only one landmark you need, beloved, and I am close beside you."

"Even in this, Lord?"

"Even in this."

Chapter Nine
Old Trunks and Other Baggage

Thirteen months after Bob and I were married, Penny joined us for a two-week Christmas visit. She brought a big tin of her delicious Danish cookies, and we both had fun baking, wrapping, and delivering cranberry loaves to friends and neighbors.

After homemade coffee cake and fresh orange juice on Christmas Day, we all gathered around the twinkling tree to open gifts. When my turn came, I eagerly unwrapped my box from Penny. Inside I found two cashmere sweaters, one beige, the other dark green. The necks in both appeared faded, the yarn thin. Each sweater had clearly been worn dozens of times. I almost cried right there beside the tree—not because I believed I was too good for her gift, but because the gift said I wasn't good enough.

"I can get others," she offered, undoubtedly noticing my expression.

"Oh, no . . ." I stammered. "Thank you. They're just what I needed. . . ."

Neither Penny nor I talked that day about my strange

present, or ever mentioned it again. Although she sometimes sent things probably bought with me in mind, from that Christmas Day I was wary. Over the years my caution proved an ongoing protection.

Numerous used purses (with face powder still clinging to the inside corners), old belts, and blouses handed down to Penny by her friends were in turn handed down to me. I gave most of them away, except for a pink quilted robe. Penny explained that "a friend gave it to me, but I don't like the color." I love pink, and wore it for years.

When caregiving begins, your loved one isn't the only thing that moves in with you. Every single piece of emotional baggage from your past relationship moves in also. It's easy to overlook those stained old suitcases in the early months of caregiving. After all, Mom or Dad is so needy now . . . and all that earlier trouble is past. Besides, everyone is telling you what a beautiful thing you're doing, and you want to believe it. But deep down, you don't.

"I didn't know how this was going to work," remembers Donna Ring when she began care for her mother-in-law. "She had been so difficult for so many years. I was willing to give it a good try for as long as possible, but I also knew I had to have help."

Old Trunks

Many caregiving relationships are positive, loving, and healthy. But just as many are not. Penny's and mine fit the latter category.

"Take care of my boy," she had whispered to me as her forty-year-old son and I left on our honeymoon. Taking care of him with all the love I knew how to give was a joy. But convincing Penny I knew what I was doing became an ongoing project. When Bob and I married, I was a divorced woman, profoundly grateful to God for the gift of our love. Bob was also divorced, but it wasn't the same: he was her son.

From the day Penny and I met, she had made it clear I didn't fit her blueprint for the ideal daughter-in-law. The

144

two of us were as different as Scottish oatmeal and Spanish salsa. Her clothes were tailored—beige or pale blue. Mine were bright plaids and Mexican pink, comfortable and casual. She made friends cautiously, over a year or two. I'd inherited the genes of my Irish grandfather who rode the bus to town one summer afternoon and returned three hours later announcing with delight, "I made a new friend today!"

I worked hard to be a good daughter-in-law, writing often, sending little gifts, supplying snapshots. Penny, too, wrote often. But nearly all her letters centered around a barely concealed hint or criticism she referred to as "just a suggestion." Bob and I knew those suggestions were transparent attempts to conform our lives to her ideas.

"How much money did you give John for the movie?" she asked me during one of her visits as our ten year old left for a matinee.

"He earned the money for his admission," I said proudly. "And I gave him fifty cents for treats."

"You shouldn't do that, you know."

I said nothing, but I remember my anger. She had raised her child. Now it was my turn.

"It's not good for the children to drink skim milk," she told us during another visit. A few weeks later a check arrived, tucked inside a note suggesting we switch to whole milk instead of skim. We sent it back with a warm note of "Thanks, but no thanks." I loved Penny, but I would not allow her to control me or our family.

Those experiences were hard. She told us in a hundred subtle ways how we should do things, and why. Rarely did she offer any praise. I felt I had been examined and rejected, and would never measure up to Penny's expectations.

Then caregiving began, and overnight, the distance between us shrank to fifteen feet. The problem was that all my memories *didn't* shrink. On the surface I was friendly and kind. But my anger grew as Penny passively accepted my diapering her, serving her meals, and reordering my entire life around her every necessity.

145

I sensed that she had achieved her goal. Although physically helpless, she now dominated every part of our household. Of course I knew she couldn't help it. Of course I knew she'd change it in a second if she could. But though I wanted her with us, I couldn't forget how she had treated me. That emotional baggage from the past soon cluttered the present.

As I sought to prayerfully identify with Penny, I tried to dig beneath the surface facts. Who and what had really formed my mother-in-law? It didn't take long to realize we knew surprisingly little about her—only bits and snippets gleaned during her Christmas and summer visits.

Her mother, Patharine Christensen, had immigrated to America from Denmark in her late teens. Penny spoke often and lovingly of her. Patharine married a mining engineer, William Edward Pentecost. They had two children: Penny, whose given name was Hazel, and a younger brother, Virgil.

Patharine raised her only daughter with old country love blended with a stoic strictness. She exalted self-control above all other virtues. One Thanksgiving when Patharine was living with Bob and his mother, she fell while waiting for them on the front porch. As they enjoyed the holiday dinner at a friend's home, she said nothing about it. After they returned home four hours later, Patharine complained that her arm was throbbing and asked Penny to help her unbutton and take off her dress. An X-ray early the next morning revealed a fractured wrist.

In addition to self-control, Patharine schooled her daughter in the things she felt a proper young lady should know and do. Penny was baptized and helped to memorize the Lord's Prayer, a fact Bob discovered years later as they prayed together in our home each night. Every Saturday, no matter what the weather, Penny was instructed to go outside and brush her beautiful long hair 200 strokes. More than eighty years later, she almost purred when we brushed her hair morning and night.

Patharine taught her daughter to keep a watchful ear on everything she said, and Penny grew up guarded in speech. She told me many times, "Of the unspoken word you are master, but the spoken word is master of you." That's good advice I'm still working on. It was fun to talk with her about everyday events, but she was ill at ease whenever feelings were expressed. When that happened, she usually bolted from the room, coughing. Some of her behavior was due to the era when she grew up, but a great deal of it she learned from her mother.

Patharine developed her needlework to an art form. We treasure several sets of her exquisite pillowcases, trimmed with three inches of dainty, intricate crochet work. She began teaching her daughter to sew when Penny was seven years old, and before long assigned her first project: hemming a handkerchief.

Penny described to us how hard she worked before she felt her handkerchief was good enough to show to her mother. But the stitches were too big, so Patharine told her to remove them and do it over. The little girl did as she was instructed, carefully rehemming the small square. Again the stitches failed in size. Patharine finally accepted the work on Penny's seventh attempt.

As a tiny boy Bob called Patharine "Granny," and was dressed in her beautifully knit sweaters, soakers, and suits. Penny told me that her mother knitted or crocheted constantly. Because of that, Penny trained herself to rest her hands in her lap and do nothing. She never failed to repeat that story on the rare occasions I found time to pick up one of my own knitting projects.

We could unearth very little about Penny's father, and unless we questioned her, she never talked about him. But when she did, she prefaced her words by saying with love in her voice, "he was very handsome." We learned he was born in College Corner, Ohio, and became a mining engineer. After he and Patharine married, he moved his young family to Spokane, then a hub of turn-of-the-century mining.

We knew Penny's mother had been alone for many years, though Penny never explained why. In later years, Patharine alternated living with Virgil and Penny. She finally died, almost eighty, in a Los Angeles nursing home. After Penny's Phoenix home was sold, we came across papers in the back of a bureau drawer that confirmed the sadness we had long suspected: William Pentecost had left Patharine, Penny, and Virgil. Not long after, he remarried.

Our attempts to learn something about Virgil also met a dead end. Penny and her brother long ago had a falling-out over their mother's care, and Penny refused to talk to him or about him. Then late one summer afternoon she turned to Bob and said, "There's something you should know. Your Uncle Virgil died." Bob knew next to nothing about his uncle, and had no idea he was sick. Penny sought out no details, and did not attend her brother's funeral.

She had graduated from the University of California at Berkeley, trained to teach learning disabled children. Later Penny married a young Phoenix attorney, Robert Henry Armstrong. They had one child, my husband Bob. But eleven years later her marriage failed, though Penny's stacks of yellowed letters testified to her ongoing efforts to restore their home. In the years that followed, Penny owned and operated a fine dress shop, and combined her considerable homemaking skills with philanthropic work.

Other Baggage

Though Penny and I talked often during her visits, I always sensed a kind of barrier between us. It was as though the real Penny, the one I wanted so much to know, was hiding. She would discuss recipes and children, her son and grandchildren, for hours. But if anything more personal came up, she'd give a polite reply, change the subject, or have a coughing spasm.

It wasn't long before I reached a conclusion: Penny didn't want to be close to me, because I wasn't what she thought I should be. I longed for her to love me for who I was, not simply tolerate me because her son had married me. Although I was always polite, our relationship wasn't helped by my firm rejection of her continued efforts to control me.

As the years passed, I nurtured the superficial, luke-warm bond between us. But deep down, I came to grips with the fact that for some reason which I could not under-stand or change, Penny and I would never be truly close. My sense of her personal rejection manifested itself in a clutter of other baggage all too familiar to most caregivers.

Anger and its close cousin, bitterness, are perhaps the most common baggage of caregiving, though these feelings are usually denied. They spring from the varied soil of any caregiving relationship: an adult child angry at an aging parent, a well spouse angry and bitter about the other's sickness, even a parent angry about a child's chronic illness.

"The need for encouragement is common among care-givers who have few happy memories of the patient— even *before* caregiving," writes Geneva Canada. "Everything, if you are not on guard, brings such unpleasant memories of the past. In other words, *bitterness.*"

"We are working on not being bitter," shared Mary Lou Sprowle. "It would only destroy ourselves."

"As caregiving began," remembers a wife whose hus-band has senile dementia, "I was angry first with his dis-ease, then about my role. I had gone through 25 years of my husband's alcoholism, and eighteen years of depression."

One man, now in mid-life, remembers being three years old when his parents emphasized that he must honor and obey them over everything else. They also stressed that Jesus was coming back someday, and that if Jesus came back while he wasn't obeying them, the little boy would not go to heaven. "It scared me to death," he said, "and I obeyed. But my anger grew and grew. I'm learning to deal with it, but . . . ." The roots of this man's anger, along with thousands of others, stretch all the way back to earliest childhood.

In addition to anger and bitterness, the grief most care-givers feel could be crammed into dozens of old suitcases. They grieve on many levels, often unaware of most of them. Caregiver grief originates in the progressive losses taking place in their lives.

The person's prior relationship with the loved one often becomes a poignant loss. Every time she visits or cares for her relative, it invisibly resurfaces. Perhaps she sees Mom, who efficiently raised thousands of dollars each year for the civic symphony, chatting for hours with imaginary friends on an unconnected phone. Or her dad, unable to speak, stares at her in silent supplication, his whiskered cheeks glistening with tears. The caregiver's loss and grief defy words.

The spouse caregiver copes with the most complicated, and possibly most painful, grief of all. He or she is losing a friend, lover, sharer of youth, helper, confidant, protector, and advocate. But it is not an abrupt, searing loss. It burns on, through months and years, slowly intensifying. When the loved one ceases to recognize the caregiver, or emotional, verbal, or physical abuse takes place, grief inundates the person. She must cope not only with the demands of the present, but also with the memories of what once was.

And every caregiver, whatever her relationship with the loved one, grieves for her own life. As we have already seen, much of what she treasured in the relationship will be boxed up and stored away. It is an ongoing loss, but a caregiver has little choice. She is torn: devoted to her parent, spouse, or whoever is needing her, yet longing to be fully herself.

Even more old baggage contains guilt, and its stepchild, shame. Guilt is like a dandelion: indiscriminate in its choice of soil, deep-rooted, and tenacious once sprouted. Though guilt burrows its roots into almost any emotion the caregiver may feel, it thrives in the loam of anger.

"I kept the family and friends unaware of my problems," recounted Marian Mills, "which was possible because my husband's social skills remained. I couldn't understand his personality changes. I felt frustrated and guilty."

Almost every caregiver creates unrealistic and often impossible self-expectations. Friends, neighbors, and family laud her sacrificial attitudes. But without adequate help and support, she becomes an emotional whirlpool, loathing much of what she must do. She knows all too well that she is not the wonderful person everyone tells her she is. Like bloodhounds, shame and guilt trail her daily journey.

"I often hope and pray that the Lord will allow my mother to pass quietly in her sleep," confides Barbara Eagan. "I feel that if she cannot again be whole that I would like to see her freed from the unhealthy shell of her body and mind. I sometimes feel guilty for feeling that way. I know I would miss her if she were gone, but I feel that parts of my mother are already dead."

Caregivers must frequently tiptoe around emotional baggage tagged not with their own names, but with their relatives'. One of the principal methods Penny used in dealing with life was denial. "I have trained myself never to think about anything unpleasant," she told me on many occasions. This meant she had literally forgotten the dates of her parents' births and deaths, the year she graduated from college, her son's age, her own age, how long she had lived in Phoenix, and much more.

As most of life involves things less than ideal, extracting accurate information about Penny's past, or her present, proved a real challenge. Her all-inclusive denial meant she truly believed she could walk anywhere she wanted to go, would get better and better, and before long could drive her car again. She needed and wanted no help whatsoever.

"Mary, you know that girl who was here this morning?"

"Yes," I answered, turning off the vacuum cleaner. "She's a nurse's aide."

"Well, she says she's coming back this afternoon."

"She is—to help you get ready for dinner."

Her lips tighten. "I don't need anybody."

"Yes, you do. And I need her help, too."

"Well, she's not coming!"

And since Penny denied having birthdays, celebrating them called for imagination.

"How was your birthday, Penny?"

She paused. "I didn't have a birthday."

"How was your chocolate cake?"

"Wonderful!"

Someone has said that aging people become more and more what they were all along. The negative, critical person complains, is impossible to please, and cares little about anyone but himself. The cheerful, appreciative, interested person asks about others, laughs, and means it when he says "thank you" and "please." Because denial helped Penny cope with the difficult parts of her early life, it became more important to her as time passed. My challenge wasn't to change that: it was to work my way around it.

The heaviest, most difficult emotional baggage for caregivers is depression. It creeps onto the luggage ramp slowly, usually after months or years of anger, grief, guilt, and bitterness.

"When caregiving began," wrote Barbara, "I felt overwhelmed and depressed. I have to constantly fight feelings of depression when I see my mother or think of her condition. Looking into my mother's eyes is very painful. I am doing better but need to keep working on it."

"I was deeply saddened by the deterioration of my parents, and frustrated by the tremendous amount of time consumed," a caregiver for both parents recalls. "I felt increased anxiety with recurring emergencies."

Another shared that "contending with the irritability and depression of my husband was the hardest part of caregiving. We had just gotten used to one year of retirement, and here was 'the rest of our lives.' Retiring from my 'solo' social life was also very hard."

Caregiver depression, whenever it surfaces, cries out for help. If you're struggling with it, resolve today to fight for yourself. Call your doctor and make an appointment, or ask him or her for a referral to someone else. Set up a meeting with your minister. Gather what little strength you've got left, and get some help. Today.

Anger, bitterness, grief, rejection, guilt, loneliness, shame, denial, and depression are heavy, cumbersome baggage. They slow your progress, weigh you down, hold you back, mar holidays and celebrations, and discolor the past, present, and future. And they weigh even more when your relative says things that hurt you, whether or not the hurt is intentional.

"She is very demanding and able to get around, but refuses to," confided Mary Lou Sprowle. "She sits in her room all day, except for meals, which must be on time. She talks loudly to herself, discussing all of us and her feelings toward us. If I leave someone else in charge in order to get out, she complains when I return. She is always with me. No matter where I go, no matter what I do, there she is. I had to go to our doctor last week. He said I was under too much stress and told me to get rid of it . . . ?"

Perhaps you're lugging around some caregiver baggage, and longing to set it down. Do you nourish ancient grudges? Do you find it hard to relax around your relative? Do you mentally rehearse unpleasant scenes to support your cause? Do you avoid your loved one's room? Or if you're there, do you edge toward the door? Do you smother Mom with excessive attention? Is it hard for you to hug dear old Dad?

If you answered yes to some of those questions, you're probably wearing yourself out with excess baggage. Don't give up. No matter how corroded, moldy, and worn your old trunks and other baggage may be, you can get rid of them.

In the Market for a Baggage Dump?

As my caregiving season with Penny continued, so did my anger and hurt. Over and over I prayed for release. I forgave Penny, and asked God to forgive me for anything I had done to hurt her. Bob and I talked about all this over coffee and many an English muffin, and his unqualified love and endless understanding did much to strengthen me. Patient, faithful friends listened and wrote me as I fought to break free of the past's tangled strands.

Finally, with Bob's encouragement, I made an appointment with our Anglican priest, Father Robert Creech. In his office early one October morning, I poured out the entire story. I wept in sorrow for the love I believed my mother-in-law refused to give. Nothing I did ever seemed good enough for her, I explained. It helped to know Bob felt the same way, yet that still did not bring the deep release my soul longed for. As I talked, I realized that on top of all my other feelings, I was also afraid of Penny.

"I've forgiven her over and over," I explained, pulling my third tissue from a nearby box. "But I can't seem to forget what she's done—or not done. I want to, but I can't. What's wrong with me?"

He leaned forward and smiled. "There's nothing wrong with you. You've identified how she hurt you, and you've forgiven her. That's very clear. Now you need to give God time to heal you from those bitter memories. As you leave the whole thing with Jesus, the hurt will slowly go away. Let Him deal with it. You don't need to anymore."

"Healing?" I asked. I'd thought forgiveness was enough. Besides, if anyone needed healing it was Penny, not I.

"Emotional healing is a process," Father Creech told me. "I want you to begin to concentrate on the cross of Christ, and on what God did there for you and for Penny. As time passes, you'll focus less and less on what she did to you. Why don't we pray about it right now?"

We prayed together in his quiet office, while a misty autumn rain crept down the paned window. No lightning bolts streaked across the grey sky, but I left his office changed. In the months that followed, my love for Penny grew—slowly and imperceptibly. My memories didn't go away. Instead, a new understanding wrapped around them.

I had invited Jesus Christ into my life when I was twenty years old. I didn't know very much about the Bible then. But I surrendered my heart to Jesus in tender response to the unconditional love He showed me through His death on the cross. After an evening Bible study in my nursing school dorm, I knelt by my bed on the sixth floor and turned my life over to Jesus.

Many things happened after that, including marriage, three little boys, a divorce, and the death of my five-year-old middle son from leukemia. I continued to grow in my faith, finding God more than sufficient for every pain and sorrow I experienced.

Penny was the first person I'd known that I couldn't seem to get close to. She had invited Christ into her own life during a prayer at a Christmas luncheon. I had hoped that glorious shared reality would be a fresh bond between us. But her faith, like her past, remained a private, closed matter.

Still I yearned for her love and acceptance, perhaps in part to fill the void left by my own mother's death four years earlier. Her Scotch-Irish makeup had sprinkled my days with joy, like the morning she climbed down from a ladder and lowered one leg—shoe, sock, and all—into a pail of sudsy water. I waited, not sure how to respond, until she burst into peals of laughter.

I'd knocked all around the edges of the sealed windows of Penny's life, but couldn't pry them open. Eventually, I stopped trying. I began caregiving with a willing and wide-open heart, forgiving her in prayer but deep down, still hurting. As she became more passive and dependent, my old anger bubbled close to the surface. I was guilty, frustrated, and defeated.

My healing that began that October morning wasn't an overnight phenomenon. It was a turning point, the beginning of wholeness. As the winter slipped by, I gained a new perspective on God's transforming power to heal. But not in Penny's life. In mine.

In prayer, step by tiny step, I retraced the long path to her childhood. I felt her fear as she pressed the covers against her ears, shutting off her parents' angry voices. I imagined the sound of her mother's lonely crying in the night. I let myself feel the pain of the girl with thick, blonde hair growing up without the handsome father she adored.

I sensed her creative spirit bound by a frightened mother determined to prepare her daughter for life—even when that meant hemming a handkerchief seven times in one day. I understood Penny's abandonment as written pleas to her tall, lanky husband failed to bring him home again. The little girl, deserted by her father, was to raise her own son without his.

That rejection by father and husband drove Penny to take fierce, desperate control of everyone and everything in her life. She resolved never to be dependent on anyone for her welfare, a goal she achieved until her last years. But like sticky tentacles, her need for protective control crept beyond her own life into everyone around her.

Into my recognition of these facts and feelings God poured a new love. Penny's need to control would not change, and it didn't matter. Jesus alone was in control, and because of Him I could simply let it go. I could stare straight into the past and understand, and love her even more.

Perhaps the person you are caring for has hurt you. Your relationship may contain no giant fissures, but it isn't what you'd hoped for and emotional baggage you're not proud of is piling up.

Or maybe your father's very life now depends on you, but he criticizes everything you do for him. And your searing pain goes back to the earliest years, when as a little child you longed for the love he never gave.

Or perhaps your relationship with your husband has been substandard for years. Illness, addictions, or long seasons of neglect have drained the desire and love you once felt. Yet today he cannot walk without your strong shoulder under his, cannot eat without splattering food all over his stylish jumpsuit. You are angry, bitter, and so very, very tired.

Or maybe you must care for a mother or mother-in-law who wrote you off many years ago. Your life went on, but your inner soul still listened for the phone calls, hoped for the tiny gifts, and looked for the cards that never came. Now she needs you as you once needed her, and your resentment is ocean deep.

On and on and on goes the litany. Deep into the murky past it runs, cutting across the fiber of your heart. There is a place of healing; there is a time; there is a way. The place is where you will not be disturbed. The time is now. The way is Jesus.

Begin, beloved, by acknowledging exactly how your relative has hurt you. Do this by yourself, or with your minister, priest, friend, or counselor. Stop making excuses for this one who has so blunted the tenderness you used to feel. Even if your loved one professes faith in Christ, list before God all the pain you have felt at his or her hand. Take your time, and whisper it all to Him. Don't hold back. Family members do hurt us in very real, painful ways—on purpose or not.

Pour out the resentments you feel, as I did about Penny's "suggestions." I loathed them. I wanted her to love me for myself, not for how close I might come to being a carbon copy of her. This process of confession will be excruciating if you do it slowly and correctly. And it is essential for healing.

Next, close your eyes and take a long, inward look at the cross of Christ. As it looms before you, imagine the agony Christ endured as the full weight of His strong body slumped against the crude, hammered nails. Bow low to the ground, and with all the love welling up inside you, thank Him for what He bore in your place.

With your eyes still closed, stand there at the foot of the cross, and think of the person who has so hurt you. Before Jesus, thank Him for His love for both of you. Open your fists and your heart, and release to Jesus every hurt, every pain, every mean word, and every unlovely characteristic of the one beside you. Last of all, yield to Him the sin of your own unforgiveness.

Give everything to Christ, who will take it all to the Father. Let it go, and with it your secret role of judge. God alone is judge. Jesus Christ has done it all, and He will bring healing to your relationship in ways you cannot now imagine.

Invite Jesus to fill you with Himself, perhaps for the very first time, anew and afresh. Concentrate on Him, and on the cross. Tear up all the old lists of your relative's offenses against you. Give everything from the past to Jesus. He will deal with it. Go forth a changed person.

From this moment on, accept the one who hurt you exactly as he or she is. Draw from God a fresh love for that person—a perspective you've never had before. Some of your hurts from the past may be so grievous they demand counseling. If so, seek out that extra help, using today's prayer as a new beginning. Let the cross become the center of your caregiving relationship, not all the pain you felt for so long. And when the cross is truly at the center, everything is made new. Praise and thank God for restoring you fully as a family, and for making you whole at last.

Now begins the exciting opportunity of allowing Christ to love your relative through you. Don't expect any change in his or her response. Your loved one hasn't had the experience of release and healing that you have had. You may someday be free to share it. But until then, your job is to love, without agenda and without expectation. Because of Christ's love for you both, you can love your relative. Trust the Holy Spirit to continue to work in every part of your caregiving ministry.

Many wonderful things happened as God healed Penny's and my relationship. Did He give me amnesia? No. If I chose to, I could still wallow in the old pain. I chose not to. Instead, I consciously worked on seeing first the cross, then Penny. Jesus loved her enough to create her, then give His life for her—just as He did for me. What love! With that example and focus, releasing the past became easier each day.

My caregiving journal expanded visibly during this time of healing. Day after day I poured out my feelings, often with tears in place of the old bitterness. It became easier to talk to Penny, and I learned how to help her laugh. Her smiles had always seemed forced to me, but as I relaxed, so did she.

We talked about her Phoenix home, ignoring the fact that it was sold. When she forgot things or announced she'd soon be well enough to move back, I smiled and let it go. We talked about the dress shop she had enjoyed running so much, the teacher's training she never used, and the reasons why. The more we talked, the more I understood and cared. God had freed me to remain separate from Penny, yet be a part of her. The healing was complete.

My spirit soared one afternoon as I introduced Penny to a nurse who was there to check her blood pressure. Penny smiled up at me, then turned to the stranger. "We have someone real special here," she announced. "Her name is Mary."

God's grace had washed over us both.

"Father, I feel like a Christmas ornament that once was beautiful, before it fell to the floor and shattered. Remembering what happened hurts so much . . . ."

"Place My cross between you and the past, my child. I will bring healing, and make you whole again."

"Even in this, Lord?"

"Even in this."

Chapter Ten

Nice People Don't Think Those Thoughts

Penny had been with us almost two years when a winter flu outbreak hopscotched its way through Spokane. Though she had always had excellent immunity, we did our best to protect her from it. Yet a few days after the new year she developed a worrisome cough. Dr. Craig prescribed an antibiotic and ordered a humidifier set up in her room, frequent changes of Penny's position, and lots of liquids.

But twenty-four hours later, she was in trouble: extremely pale with shallow, rapid breathing and a fever of 101. Dr. Craig ordered oxygen and arranged to come to our home the next day. She arrived in the midst of a heavy, wet snowfall. After examining Penny, she prescribed a different antibiotic.

Bob had taken an hour off for the doctor's visit, and after the examination the three of us sat down for a cup of coffee in the kitchen. Apprehensive, Bob and I asked if his mother should be hospitalized.

"Considering her age," Dr. Craig answered, "nothing would be done in a hospital that you aren't doing at home. Her care is superb."

Her words gave us a much-needed boost. We had sensed silent disapproval from some people because we didn't rush Penny into the hospital.

"She has bronchitis," Dr. Craig continued. "But what concerns me most is her overall lack of response. She seems to be tuned-out, which is different from her normal pattern." The doctor set her coffee cup down. "Because of her age and congestive heart failure," she said slowly, "your mother may not pull out of this."

Once more she assured us that a hospital could offer no more care than what Penny was receiving at home. She urged us to leave her alone for short periods (in bed, with the side rails up), if we needed to run to the store.

"Just go about your business," she encouraged us. "This is a part of life."

We'll never forget Dr. Craig's support and common sense, or the compassion that brought her to our home in the middle of a winter storm.

By the next night we were sure Penny was slipping away. She was almost impossible to wake up, chewed the straw I offered to her, and carried on rambling conversations with somebody named Johnson. She couldn't follow commands, even "lift up your right hand," despite three or four repetitions.

During all this, Bob and I were up several times each night to sponge Penny's dry, hot face, spoon water into her mouth, reassure her, and move her from side to side so fluid didn't pool in her lungs. She kept pulling the oxygen tube from her nose, and we had to replace it about every two hours.

For the first time since her arrival, she wasn't able to pray one word of the Lord's Prayer with Bob. He held her hand and prayed for both of them.

For four weeks Penny struggled to return to normal. One morning about halfway through that time, the nurse's aide and I managed to lower her into the recliner. She remained there for several hours, surrounded by blankets, shawls, and soft pillows.

Penny slept almost all day for many weeks, her mouth wide open, her lips sagging around her few remaining teeth. Often I'd look in from the hall and wonder if she were still alive. She was, and continued to push herself to regain strength. Little by little, she succeeded.

When Death Doesn't Come

During this crisis, Bob and I were completely worn out. One day we would think Penny was passing away, but the next we weren't so sure. Then the cycle repeated. We discovered that waiting for a death that didn't come extracted all our energy. We felt as if we were riding a medical roller coaster. One week we expected Penny to die at any moment. The next she'd be watching "Little House on the Prairie." Many caregivers have walked that thin line between two worlds: loving their relative even while hoping for his—and their—release.

"We wished she would die only in the sense that we knew she could not get well. We did not want her to suffer," remembers Dean Price about his mother-in-law. "We had heard that she could linger for a long time, and this *was* a concern."

During Penny's illness we prepared easy-to-digest, nutritious meals. We encouraged and comforted her. But at the same time we yearned for the day it would all be over—for her and for us. *If only we were free from the responsibility of her welfare. If only we could stop fearing she was worse. If only we could have our house back, the rooms freed of cumbersome equipment, the endless washing ended. If only Bob could come home from work and do nothing more than read the paper.* Nice people do, most certainly, think those thoughts. We considered ourselves nice people; we were thinking those thoughts—and we were ashamed.

Other caregivers struggle in different ways. "I wished sometimes she would go away or back upstairs," said Donajeanne Bogart. "But never die!"

Geneva Canada commented that, "As of the last few weeks, I have mixed feelings!"

163

"I never wished he would die," wrote Carolyn. "I *did* wish he would stay in bed and sleep."

Yet countless caregivers, at one time or another, wish their relative were dead, that the ordeal would be all over.

"I have wished Mom would die," wrote Ted Hutchinson, "and so has she. She often complains of life and wishes she could die. I'm pretty guarded about who I admit that to, because it's so unspiritual. At the bottom line lies the awareness that the thought or feeling is pretty selfish. But life would be easier; we wouldn't have to deal with inconvenience or hassles or unpleasantness. There would be one less concern for the future, and it would be more convenient. Yet who says life is supposed to be easy?"

"I wished many times she would die," admitted Mary Lou Sprowle, "especially after a very difficult time of family tension. Or perhaps when important things were coming up, and I knew we could not participate. To be honest, I thought one morning I would walk into her room and she would have died during the night, bringing an end to my misery and hers. It just didn't happen."

Mary Lou continued, "I thought I was the only person to feel or think these things. I thought I was a Christian, a strong one at that, who could handle anything and always do right. I wished for her death, and my halo fell off, so to speak. I was in deep depression near the end."

"I also wished she would die," added Mary Lou's husband David. "Then we'd be free again. I feel bad about those thoughts. A son should not have those thoughts about his mother—or anyone else."

When you wish for your loved one's death, a host of too familiar feelings aren't far behind. Probably the most frequent reaction is relentless, self-accusing guilt.

"I wished he would die," confided a caregiver about her husband, "and then I would have horrible guilt feelings."

Another wrote that "I only wished she would die at the very last. When she labored so hard to breathe, it was terrible. I couldn't help her, and I felt guilty."

Anger also works its devious way into the guilt picture, stirring the already bubbling emotional pot. Jane Hutchinson admits, "I have recently wished she would die. I think wistfully about what freedom would be like, and consciously try not to dwell on it. I dislike those thoughts, but am learning to deal with anger legitimately, rather than 'stuffing' it inside, though."

As we have seen, grief is the omnipresent ingredient in caregiving. The sense that death is not far off adds to the many levels of loss discussed earlier. An approaching death brings that reality into an uncomfortable, too-bright focus, as though looking at it through a child's kaleidoscope.

Last of all, dressed as usual in many disguises, comes denial. A single caregiver, desperate for release, wishes her loved one would die. Then drowning in guilt, she buries the hated thought in a hurricane of care for her relative. Excessive activity is a common disguise for denial, recognized only by the seasoned caregiving veteran.

With husband-and-wife caregiving teams, denial sometimes adopts another camouflage. One spouse may accept a loved one's approaching death, while the other denies it. He or she refuses to go to any funerals, cannot verbalize or acknowledge the terminal illness or death of friends, and cannot make any of the decisions mandated by the end of a life. That kind of denial by half of a caregiving team erects invisible barriers around an approaching death.

Survival Key #1: Acceptance

Maybe you've been a caregiver for a very long time, or possibly not long at all. But recently, from time to time, you've wished that death, sometimes called the old man's friend, would come. You've nursed your relative through a host of medical crises, and nursed him well—so well that he survived, the emergency leveled off, and you find yourself once again gliding over a level stretch of the caregiving roller coaster. You know it's only a matter of time before the whole thing plunges downward again. You wish the ride would end, and you are swamped with guilt.

You are neither morbid nor monstrous. You're entirely normal. Every caregiver from the beginning of time has felt exactly as you do. The only difference is whether or not they admitted their feelings. The healthiest thing you can do is express what you feel and accept those feelings as part of caregiving. Welcome to the ranks. You're one of millions who have been there—and understand.

You also need to zealously guard against getting too absorbed with your relative's death. As we've detailed already, maintain an outside interest, even as death draws near. If you sense depression settling around you, don't run for cover. Run for help.

Most important of all, talk over your loved one's eventual death with someone you completely trust. Say what you feel. Use the words you usually shy away from. Be brutally honest. Work your way through the underbrush of emotions until you find the serenity of acceptance. Your caregiving season *will* end in death, whether it takes place in your home or somewhere else. That unavoidable finality is one reason your ministry is so terribly difficult.

Talk about your loved one's disease, helplessness, problems related to care, and every facet of your situation. If you need to, repeat the steps to achieve healing of a specific area (discussed in Chapter 9). Then, as you accept God's timing for your loved one's death, receive today as His very special gift to both of you. And resolve to make it the most beautiful day you can.

Survival Key #2: Planning

Grab hold of acceptance—it's a sturdy handle on one side of the medical roller coaster. On the other side you'll find another handle: planning. If your loved one has made his wishes known regarding the funeral, you'll need only to see that those desires are carried out. Or perhaps, as was true with Penny, death is a subject your relative is unable to discuss. You may have no idea of his or her preferences.

In that case, the place to begin is with your doctor. Our discussion with Dr. Craig during Penny's bronchitis was very frank. It was then we decided, with the doctor's agreement, not to use extraordinary means to prolong Penny's life. We were, and are, strongly opposed to hastening death by any method whatsoever. Yet death was inevitable, and as it approached we wanted no breathing machines, gastric tubes, or midnight ambulance rides to force her worn-out heart to further, short-lived service.

Dr. Craig listened to our wishes, and all three of us reviewed how we would handle Penny's death when the time came. First, we would stay in close touch with the doctor. Second, we would continue to feed Penny water and nourishing foods. But if the day came when she could no longer open her mouth or swallow, we would not begin intravenous or tube feedings. We understood that as natural death approaches, all systems of the body slow down. Forcing food and fluids into it through artificial means only drags out the process.

Third, we agreed that should Penny's breathing stop, we would not revive her with CPR, and we wanted nobody else to do so. Dr. Craig signed a paper provided by our agency to this effect. We taped it to the inside of a kitchen cupboard and made sure every aide read and understood it.

Last of all, we decided to give Penny antibiotics and oxygen as needed for shortness of breath and any infections. We would, of course, give her all of her regular prescribed medications. But when she could no longer take them by mouth, even crushed and diluted with yogurt and fruit juice, we would not switch to injections. We reached these decisions recognizing that she was ninety years old, and at the natural close of her life. Illuminating our thinking was the Bible's glorious promise that to be away from the body is to be at home with the Lord (II Corinthians 5:8).

Penny had recovered from her very serious infection, but never to the level of wellness she had enjoyed before. Yet that experience forced us, with Dr. Craig's wise counsel, to face the fact that Penny's death probably wasn't far off. We made deeply personal decisions, and reached agreement on all of them. Though we did not want Penny to die, we realized it was almost time. And we were ready.

Dr. Craig also urged us to select a funeral home. Father Creech suggested one, and Bob talked by phone with its director. We had long ago decided to have Penny cremated, with her ashes buried in the secluded and peaceful rose garden behind our church.

There was little more we could do at this point, other than to keep the funeral home's number near the phone. When death occurred, one call to the director would take care of everything else. As had been true in talking to Dr. Craig, making arrangements for Penny's death was a practical help and emotional relief.

"Preplanning the funeral and removal of the body is important," emphasizes Glenna Mills. "Also, if autopsy or other medical study is anticipated, this must be done in advance."

The Vigil

Eight months after John and Rita's wedding, we experienced the joy of another. Our youngest son, Matthew, and his Lori were married in late May of the following year. Because Lori's large family lived in Oregon, we carved out two full weeks to enjoy the wedding celebration and a much-needed vacation. Since our caregiving began, we had been away only a few days at a time. A two-week rest sounded too good to be true.

It required months of planning to leave Penny with a carefully screened nurse's aide from a local agency. We set out and labeled each day's supply of pills. I typed long lists detailing her routine, needs, preferences, and problems. We spelled out our exact itinerary, what the cats needed, who would walk the dog, how to run the washer and drier, and what to do if anything went wrong along the way.

In our memories, that trip will always remain in timeless suspension. Our souls were restored by nights of long, uninterrupted sleep, hours and hours together with nothing more to do than plan our next stop, and the ongoing pre-wedding excitement. On Matt's and Lori's wedding day, Oregon's misty skies parted like a curtain. Shimmering sunlight sparkled over the lavender, seafoam green, and coral hues of bridesmaids' gowns and the satin ribbons of Lori's gardenia bouquet.

God used those two weeks to prepare us for what lay ahead. After we arrived home, though the aide had taken outstanding care of Penny, we were alarmed at her change in only fourteen days. She was becoming increasingly short of breath, requiring oxygen to be helped into and out of bed. Her diapers, always soaked during the night, now were often dry. Her twenty-four hour intake of liquids decreased steadily.

As May blended into June, then June into July, Penny seemed to pull steadily inward. She had needed to be fed since the bronchitis, but by summer she could not chew the softest foods. I pored over cookbooks and devised a varied, soft diet of soups, custards, puddings, and fortified milkshakes. By the end of July she refused even those.

Though everyone who entered her room offered her water or juice, her urine grew more and more concentrated. We constantly battled to keep her skin clear of breakdowns. She slept more and more, and spoke rarely even when awake. She spit out her food and rested her hands in the middle of it if not watched. Often I found her deeply asleep, her feet and hands twitching in a strange way.

As the summer passed, everything in our lives changed as we focused more and more on Penny's approaching death. We entered a time warp of megafatigue, more profound than anything we had yet experienced. For the first time, we hit the caregiving wall. We had no energy for anything other than what was taking place in our home. Everything in our lives went on hold: guests, going out, meetings, classes, optional phone calls.

We knew Penny's death was imminent, but not when. We had heard that some home deaths come suddenly.

"My mother died quietly in bed," wrote Elizabeth Cox, "as I was out in the kitchen preparing breakfast."

"Caregiving ended with the peaceful death of my wife during her nap after breakfast," remembers Laverne Kerns.

But other deaths drag on, like a feather drifting earthward from high above. Penny's death was like that. Her appearance changed dramatically a full six weeks before she died. For so long we had checked on her through the day, and always got a smile or a wave back. It was strange to find her sleeping in the reclining chair, her mouth sunken, her eyes half closed, her breathing labored. For the first time, I noticed a faint, strange odor in her room.

But Penny was not the only one whose appearance and routine turned inside out. As July slipped into August, Bob and I found it impossible to concentrate on anything for more than a few minutes. We were always preoccupied with Penny, wondering if she needed water spooned into her mouth, her face sponged with a cloth, or additional blankets to keep her warm enough. We forgot to do things we said we would do, or mixed up the time we had agreed on.

Neither of us could sit in a chair, read, or do anything for more than a few minutes before heading to Penny's room. There was nothing to do but turn her, give her more water, keep her clean, and wait. We were both completely exhausted, but not with her physical or emotional care, which was now minimal. We were worn out with the vigil of waiting. Yet each day, God supplied exactly the energy we needed.

Many people, through word or look, told us they thought we should put Penny elsewhere. After all, it was almost over. What was all this effort for? What would be the final price tag of our caregiving? Would it affect our health? Might it affect Bob's work, or mine? We well knew it could damage both. But as the end drew near, we never once considered putting her anywhere else. After so long, it was hard to believe the time had come. But we were thankful and relieved she was with us. Death for Penny in our home felt peaceful, dignified, and right.

We encountered many people uneasy and ill at ease about our choice of a home death. They were reluctant to talk about it, and some clearly disapproved. But more supported us, asked if there were any way to help, and mailed brief notes of encouragement.

By the middle of August, Penny accepted only juice and water. Her face turned paler by the day, despite oxygen. One afternoon I walked into her room and discovered she was breathing in the way that often precedes death: about twenty seconds of no breaths, followed by twenty seconds of very slow, deep breaths that grew shallower until she reentered the no-breathing period. At this point, using a draw sheet and every ounce of strength we had, Debbi and I lifted her from the reclining chair permanently into bed.

The next day I cut two of Penny's long, flannel nightgowns from hem to neck, and stitched each raw edge. It was a sad task, but essential for her comfort, because it minimized moving her. Her urinary output had almost ceased by then, and her pale face was almost dusky. If she tried to talk, her speech was garbled. Occasionally, she managed a faint smile.

We continued to brush her beautiful hair twice a day— her mother's hair care formula was a winner. Sometimes her eyes focused on us momentarily when we spoke in a normal voice, then clouded over and closed. We kept the room quiet, the radio and television off entirely. We cleaned her mouth and teeth with glycerine sticks and little foam swabs. Because she breathed through her mouth, we coated her lips with a thin, protective layer of lubricating jelly.

The two or three weeks before Penny's death uncapped every last ounce of our caring and love. We spoke warmly to her, even when she seemed not to understand. We held her hands, stroked her forehead and arms, smiled at her, and talked briefly about happy, funny things. We kept our visits short and frequent, so as not to tire her.

We do not know if Penny realized she was dying. All her life she had chosen never to discuss death, and as her own drew near we honored her choice. Other caregivers encounter the opposite challenge: dealing with a loved one who actively desires death.

"I never wished he would die," wrote one caregiver of her partially paralyzed husband, "but it was his wish! It is one of the hardest things to contend with."

As her mother's death approached, Renée Kuehl wrote about "the obstacle we did *not* overcome: how to keep up the spirits when the care receiver no longer wanted to live. I don't think anyone has the answer for that. Mother was becoming quite annoyed with me during the last few weeks of her life—for begging her to eat, for example. It was a difficult, sad time."

For others, the approach of death offers an opportunity to fulfill promises made years before. "Young children or grandchildren who are involved in lengthy or terminal illnesses can be very positive," states Glenna Mills. "Bill and Jennifer, who were about eight and ten years old, went with me to my parents' home every weekend during my father's last year. They visited with him, watched TV, and helped with chores that he could no longer do. The last time we saw him was very special. My father had promised his mother long ago that he would join the church. Though he was a Christian, he had never formalized this promise, and it was important for my mother to see that he fulfilled it. The nuns broke the no-children-visitors rule and allowed all of us to be present in his hospital room while the Methodist minister admitted him into the church and served Communion to all of us. Following that we watched part of a football game. He died two days later."

Though Penny slept almost continually during the last few weeks of her life, Bob never missed their daily Bible reading. Keeping his voice upbeat and the Scripture passages short, he read the entire New Testament to her twice, and the Book of Psalms four times. Always he assured Penny that God was in perfect control, and loved her so very much. Though her body seemed to be almost gone, we knew her spirit received and was nourished by God's Word.

Father Creech visited Penny three hours after her pre-death breathing began. First he prayed with her, then anointed her with oil. After that she seemed to relax, breathe more calmly, and become more alert. During the days that followed, I often read a psalm to her, especially Psalm 91, a favorite of mine. After reading, I held her hand and rejoiced in God's goodness and love for her.

Three days later, the strange breathing stopped. Though it returned for short periods, her overall breathing became almost normal. At that time, with Dr. Craig's encouragement, we removed the oxygen. But each morning I hurried to her room before Bob, not wanting him to find her gone.

On Labor Day she choked on her medications and could not swallow them. I cleaned her mouth and stopped trying. It seemed strange to have so little to do, after so long. I could only change her position every two hours, rest every arm and leg on soft pillows, sponge her face, and apply lotion. I wanted to do something more to help, to make her more comfortable. But there was nothing to do. During this time we glimpsed a caregiving price tag we had never experienced: caring for a dying person in the home extracts more energy than anything that may go on before.

Later that afternoon (September 5), I could not get Penny to open her eyes. I shook her bony arm slightly and spoke her name three inches from her ear in my official nurse voice. No response, not even an eyelid twitch. She was deeply asleep, yet breathing forty times a minute. We discussed restarting the oxygen, remembered our talk with Dr. Craig, and decided against it. Had she been conscious or struggling for breath, we would have done so.

Near midnight on September 7, I stood by her bed, stroking her forehead. Her pulse was rapid and thready, and she was peacefully sleeping. Her skin felt hot, and I bathed her face, then squeezed a few drops of water from a sponge into her mouth. I stood there a long time, wondering if I should sit up with her. The end was very close, but she was unconscious. After talking it over, Bob and I decided to go to bed, leaving our bedroom door and Penny's wide open.

At 5:30 the next morning I went straight to her room. In the pale light I sensed it was over. She was in the same position I'd left her in, but cold to my touch. She'd passed away in the early morning, and all I could think of was Scripture's wondrous promise that we never die alone: angels escort believers into the presence of Christ (Luke 16:22).

I hurried back to our bedroom to tell Bob that his mother had gone Home. We wept together, prayed, and then he went in to see her. The light was up a little then, and her face was gripped in death: too pale, too set, blue. We were exhausted, but not sad. She was, at last, with Jesus.

At 6:30 we called Dr. Craig, then Father Creech. He arranged right then for a memorial service when all of our children could be with us. Last of all I called the mortuary, then went to take a shower.

As I dressed I heard Bob's voice, which seemed odd because it came from Penny's room. I hurried into the hall, and found him sitting beside her as he had done so many hundreds of times before. He was holding her hand, the Bible open in his lap, reading the Twenty-Third Psalm. "It seemed right," he told me later. If I ever had any doubts about caregiving, they disappeared at that moment.

A short time later three large men in too-tight suits arrived at the front door. One obtained details from Bob in the kitchen, while I led the others to Penny's room. Five minutes later Bob and I stood on our front walk and watched as Penny's covered body was wheeled into the van. I had thought our caregiving would never end. But right then it seemed like only a day or two, not two and a half years, since we had rushed Penny into the house after our long flight from Phoenix.

The rest of the day slipped by easily. Bob went on to work, seeking support in his routine, while I stripped Penny's bed and began the process of sorting. Before long the phone began to ring as word traveled, and soon we were surrounded by flowers, invitations to lunch, notes, offers of help, and enough food to supply several kitchens.

174

I spent the next day boxing up Penny's nighties, diapers, clothes, and everything that could be used. When Bob returned that afternoon, the room, drawers, closet, and bath were stripped of the immediate, painful memories.

That weekend, giddy with the luxury of time, we went to the County Fair. It was a turning point for us. We did nothing but eat, look at displays, watch people, and relax. The following week we continued to notify family and friends, scheduled pickups for Penny's equipment, and arranged for the badly stained carpet in her room to be cleaned.

Two weeks later the memorial service followed by a beautiful luncheon served by the women of our church demonstrated to us Christ's love poured out through His family. That weekend beloved friends brought food for each meal, including breakfast, so that we could spend every minute with Ann and Leslie, John and Rita, and Matt and Lori. It was a time of closure, and of great thanksgiving.

By Sunday evening we had waved good-bye to the last of our children and returned to our quiet house. It seemed strange not to hurry to Penny's room to visit with her, strange to have so little washing, strange not to set out her pills, strange to listen for Sherri, Pat, Debbi, Ruth, and Mary, the nurse's aides who had become such good friends. We rejoiced at Penny's release, and ours. But we missed her terribly.

"Mom always had a listening ear," remembers Donajeanne Bogart. "I miss our times together. She was fun to be with—most of the time! She found ways to minister to us also. She loved us!"

"Strangely enough," wrote Diane Price, "after she died, there were times I would have had her back—even in that condition. I missed her so!"

When caregiving ends abruptly, it takes several weeks to slow down, to realize how desperately tired you really are. But one day the funeral has come and gone. Family and friends have, for a while at least, disappeared. Plants sent in sympathy drop their once lovely blossoms. Food cooked by loving hands is gone. The house is quiet . . . much too quiet. And you feel very alone.

Suddenly you have too much time on your hands. For years you dreamed of this moment of freedom, this impossible release. Now it's here, and why aren't you excited? This is what you've waited for—but you don't feel happy, and you don't know where to start.

What's happening? You're in a grief transition, but not merely for your loved one. You grieve also for the familiar pressure of caregiving. It took months to adjust to, but eventually you did, and it carried you through the days— physical therapy, skin care, washing, bed changing, encouragement, wheelchair rides outside, midnight trips with a flashlight in case the covers slipped off Dad.

That routine pressed so hard, was so difficult. But it kept you going. And now it's gone. For a while, you may be very lonely, especially if you were a single or spouse caregiver. If you managed to preserve some of your other interests through caregiving, you won't feel such a void. Old patterns and interests will emerge. If caregiving became an all-consuming passion, you have an even more difficult job ahead: reestablishing your own life.

During your grief transition, expect memories to surface unexpectedly. I phoned Bob at work the day Penny's breathing changed so dramatically. He was working on a new office phone system, and dropped everything to rush home. Many weeks later Bob told me, "It's still hard to finish up the interrupted work on that phone system." The strong negative association made it difficult to return in any way to that sad day.

On the positive side, a home death may shorten your period of grieving. Though extremely stressful, it allows you an ongoing involvement with your loved one. Every spoonful of water, every midnight trip, every time you sponge Dad's face, you act out your grief. Most of this could be done wherever Dad is. But as a home caregiver, you carry full responsibility for everything. Strange as it seems, that heavy weight often lightens your later grieving. It may also lessen or remove guilt you might otherwise feel.

You spent yourself on your loved one for months, perhaps for years. Be patient. Give yourself two to five years to recover from one of the most difficult things you will ever do. Yes, tears will come. Yes, painful memories will blindside you when you're not looking. Yes, waves of sleepiness will wash over you during the day, cured only by the unthinkable luxury of a nap. Yield to it all. You have fought the good fight. Now it's time to rest for a while.

Let the months and years pass. Allow yourself to sleep as much as your body demands. Eat well, exercise often, and watch God's healing hand at work in your life. Let your mind wander. Do what you really want to do. And one day you'll find yourself unwrapping a box of caregiving used-to-be's and remembering. Hold them closely, and smile.

"Father, I'm frightened . . . . I don't know if I'm strong enough to see this through . . . ."

"Lean against Me, My priceless child. I will allow nothing in life or death to separate you from Me."

"Even in this, Lord?"

"Even in this."

Chapter Eleven
Forks in the Road

"**C**ould you have done this if you hadn't been a nurse?" After Penny's death, my friend's question took me by surprise. Could I?

"Yes," I told her.

I can't deny that being a nurse helped. I was well acquainted with the basics of everyday care: patient hygiene, dealing with incontinence, and knowing what problems to watch for. And as Penny's death crept closer, prior experience helped me pace myself.

But could I have done it otherwise? Unquestionably. I might have enrolled in a home nursing course or asked someone from our home-care agency to show me what I needed to know. But I'm convinced that a personal relationship with Jesus, plus a large helping of common sense, contribute far more to successful caregiving than any educational degree.

Penny's peaceful death in our home concluded Bob's and my season of caregiving. For a hundred reasons, that was a right ending for us. But for others, it isn't.

Thousands of caregivers need relief before the death of their loved one occurs. Perhaps you've reached a fork in your own road: one way leads further into caregiving, and the other goes a different direction. How do you decide which road to take? Which is right for you and your loved one?

Spotting Cracks in the Earthen Vessel

Concerning the Gospel of Christ, the apostle Paul wrote, "But we have this treasure in earthen vessels, that the surpassing greatness of the power may be of God and not from ourselves" (II Corinthians 4:7). Our bodies are the earthen vessels, and they are fragile. Under the weight of caregiving, they often develop cracks.

Some can be repaired. Others can't. But fixable or not, any fracture on the surface of your caregiving is a gracious warning from God. You need to pay attention, lest it expand and shatter you. The questions below will help you pinpoint some common weak spots that spell caution for caregivers.

- Are you losing weight, but you're not on a diet?

- Do you ever think, even briefly, of suicide?

- Do you often feel like crying?

- Are you sick too frequently? Did you know that ongoing stress lowers your resistance to infection?

- Do you fall asleep in church? In Sunday school and other classes? While driving? When you're finally in bed, is sleep the impossible dream?

- Are you uptight all the time? Does the dog's barking, children's squabbling, or the ringing of your loved one's bell drive you up the wall?

- Are you having trouble concentrating? Do you read or listen to something but can't remember it seconds later?

- Does your back hurt often?

- Do you have chronic headaches when the doctor says there's nothing physically wrong?

- Do you have diarrhea, even after tossing out all the bran and prune juice?

- Does extra pressure make your chest feel tight, even though the doctor says your heart's fine?

- Do you find it hard to express what you're really feeling?

- Are you withdrawing from life? How long has it been since you did something special with your spouse, family, or friends?

- When did you last go to church?

- Is your job suffering? How seriously?

- Do you and your family argue more and more frequently?

- Do members of your family avoid coming home?

- Are you using pills or alcohol to get through the day?

If you spotted two or more cracks in the surface of your caregiving, you need to visit a repair shop. Maybe you can fix what's wrong. Need more help? Review Chapter 5. Need to set limits? Look over Chapter 8. But maybe you uncovered some weak spots that can't be fixed—ones that are taking a toll on your own life. Maybe you've reached that fork in the road, and need to go a different direction.

Letting Go

A former caregiver confided, "I would like to have known how long to continue care and when to let go. For us, we should have let go a little sooner."

This happens all the time. Despite ominous warning signals, thousands of caregivers push themselves ever onward. Some are obsessed with a morbid preoccupation about the evils of nursing homes. Some can't let go of unrealistic and totally unworkable past promises. Others lose all touch with reality, neglect their own health, and cannot tell their relative what must be said. A few disintegrate under the strain, and end up taking their loved one's life and perhaps their own.

"Some people can handle caregiving," wrote David Sprowle, "and some can't. I couldn't. I had to learn by doing. . . . A person should think things out more. It is a serious event, one that needs thought before doing it."

"Caring was ended when Dad suffered a stroke from which he did not fully recover," wrote a caregiver of both parents. "It made home care impossible. The toughest decision we had to make was placing them both in a convalescent facility."

Is it time for you to let go of caregiving? After reviewing warning signals *you* may be experiencing, you also need to evaluate others that may affect your loved one. Caregiving is an equation that involves both you and your relative. It's possible that he or she needs something which can no longer be supplied in your home:

- Is your loved one lonely for people his or her own age?

- Is your relative too difficult, too violent, or too mean, even with medication? Some degenerative diseases, such as Alzheimer's, progress through many levels. At some of them, home care may be impossible.

- Can your loved one recognize places or people? If somebody else cared for him, would it matter?

- Does your relative require twenty-four-hour-a-day supervision, a requirement no one person can meet?

- Do you need to let go of home caregiving for your own well being, but there is nobody else to take over?

- Does your relative require treatments beyond your ability?

- Does your doctor recommend that you relinquish caregiving?

Making the Decision

When it comes to making other arrangements, David Sprowle gives good advice: "Provide the care to the best of your ability," he says, "and be ready to accept the fact that you can no longer care for a person when he or she becomes too much. When you reach the point that you can't do it anymore, *do not feel guilty* about placing the person in a care facility."

Donna Ring seconds that opinion. "I think people should not feel guilty if they have to put a family member in a convalescent hospital," she states. "The cost is terrible and they can always try home care first. But if it gets too hard, they should transfer the loved one with a free conscience."

When and if you think you may be reaching the point where home care is no longer practical, try to get some of the legwork out of the way ahead of time. If feasible, call another family conference. If that isn't possible, communicate with every family member in any of the ways suggested in Chapter 4. Also talk it over with your minister, especially if you are struggling with the decision. As with every caregiving phase, pray specifically about your search. Continue to network. Use your notebook to keep track of every suggestion and lead.

Set aside a prearranged time for a discussion with your relative's doctor, either in person or by phone. Be sure you understand exactly what your loved one needs. Should he or she be in a skilled nursing care facility? Or would an intermediate care complex meet his needs? Would he be happiest in a facility that provides limited assistance?

If you are considering a board-and-care home, make sure it's licensed. It's a good idea to check with your local public health department or the agency that licenses nursing homes in your area. Obtain a copy of the standards licensed homes must meet.

If you have worked with a home-care agency during your caregiving, or if your loved one has been in the hospital, be sure to talk with those social workers about care options. Also consider getting in touch with the hospital administrator, your attorney, and/or the Better Business Bureau. Most valuable of all, evaluate your decision with a friend—one who has been through the process, is in the midst of it, or has a relative happily settled in a local facility.

When you've done enough research, visit several of the care possibilities on your list. It's a good idea to schedule some of the visits and to drop in unannounced for others. In every place you visit, ask to see their license. Take along a small notebook to record your impressions and jot down questions.

If you find one or two facilities you especially like, arrange an appointment with the administrator. Be sure it is both Medicare and Medicaid certified. Get down to bedrock basics about cost. Have every fee spelled out: What does the basic charge cover? What doesn't it cover? What about personal laundry, haircuts and shampoos, or special meals?

Is the staff adequately trained to provide what your relative requires? Is there a registered nurse on 24-hour duty? A physician on call at all times? Are the therapy services your loved one requires available? How many beds and rooms does the facility have?

Ask to see a monthly calendar of social activities and programs. Ask about what the facility offers, such as an Alzheimer's unit, church services, bus trips, or family support groups.

As you narrow down your choice, arrange to spend some time and have a meal there. How is the food? Is it attractively served, with hot things hot and cold things cold? How do the corridors and rooms smell? Do they look clean?

Comfortable? Take a few minutes to talk to some of the residents. In another time and place, how would you feel about living there? Last of all, remember that you're not cementing your relative to the facility's floor. No matter how good it looks, start your loved one out on a trial basis if at all possible.

Tips for Caregiver Survival

It may be hard to believe, but there are some women— and men!—in this world who discover that their calling in life is caregiving. Perhaps their first exposure to it comes because a relative needs help. And before long they're remodeling their home, making its rooms as big as their hearts.

You may not be called to a ministry of perpetual caregiving. But at the same time, you've examined other options for your relative and ruled them out one by one. For better or worse, you've decided to continue. Several times Bob and I seriously considered placing Penny in a facility. We made dozens of phone calls and toured several full-care nursing homes. We spent one beautiful afternoon in a board-and-care residence where the aroma of weekly home-baked bread filled the house.

But as good as those options appeared, each time we decided against them. We would pray, talk, rearrange Penny's and our schedules a little bit, and decide to push on a while longer. If you've made up your mind to continue your caregiving ministry, maybe some of the survival techniques we discovered can help.

- Remember your priorities. (See Chapter 7.) Though caregiving may twist them like a pretzel, keep your sights on God's pattern.

- Allow nothing to come between you and your relationship with God. Each day, fight for your time with God: read His Word; pray; allow Him to meet you right where you are. No time? Get creative: pray while you're in the shower, driving to the store, or washing dishes.

Somehow, get to church on Sunday. Fill yourself up with God's love and the tangible love of His family on earth. Each day during your prayer time, make it a point to pray for caregivers around the world. Lift their needs, known and unknown, before the One who loved and loves them more than life.

- Discipline yourself to live one day at a time. This is one of the great mysteries of the Christian life: we move through it with our eyes on heaven, our hands and feet on today. Jesus taught: "Do not be anxious for tomorrow; for tomorrow will care for itself. Each day has enough trouble of its own" (Matthew 6:34).

- Nurture yourself by maintaining a part of your life separate from caregiving. Look for ways to distance yourself a little each day from your loved one, even within the same house. Keep in mind that you don't have to tell your relative everything. Nor must you drop whatever you're doing the second he or she calls.

- Join (or pray about starting) a caregiver support group.

- Treat yourself to some personal time as often as possible. As the song says, little things really do mean a lot, especially when it comes to caregiving. Do you like to do leather craft, knitting, quilting, wood carving, crochet, or ceramics? During my caregiving, knitting just one row in the car on the way home from church relaxed me.

- Discover other little things, and enjoy them. Use store perfume testers lavishly—that's what they're for. But watch out: "Midnight Madness" may not establish the mood you need to change an adult diaper. Once in a while enjoy a donut—sugar, calories, fat, and all. Relax by grooming

186

the dog, pulling weeds, inhaling deeply, or holding a baby. Keep the embers of those old loves glowing. When your caregiving season ends, they can be coaxed to flame again.

- Beg, borrow, or steal regular vacations— somehow, some way, if only for a day at a time.

- Take care of your own body. Ignore nothing. Schedule regular physical, dental, and vision checkups. Remember caregiving's axiom: Protect yourself—*you* are your loved one's most vital asset. Watch your appearance. Schedule regular haircuts, exercise sessions, and whatever else is meaningful to you.

- Don't forget to review your caregiving note-book every few weeks, especially your reasons for caregiving. Make regular entries in your journal, even when things are about the same.

- Be suspicious of any agenda other people prepare for you. Accept the fact that you can't please everyone and can't be all things to all people. Nor do you have to try.

- Expect stress to occasionally shortcircuit your memory, and don't worry about it. With rest, your mind will again function normally.

- Pray for a friend with whom you can let your hair down. Mine was Edith (mentioned in Chapter 6). A retired Nurse Anesthetist, she had already put in long years of caregiving—first for her sister, then for her dear husband. Edith often called over to me as I hung up the wash. We would sit for a half hour at her big kitchen table, drinking her wonderful coffee. Everything always looked better to me after one of our talks. A skilled, sympathetic listener, she loves to laugh and she has a streak of common sense a yard wide. Pray for such a special friend in your life. Everyone needs an Edith.

- Forget caregiving perfection. Settle for solid reality.

- Remember: caregiving *will* end. No matter how you feel today, this season in your life isn't forever.

- Scope out your local yogurt shop. What's your favorite flavor?

- Study the cat. Master the art of the catnap. Give yourself permission to turn everything off for a while. Make sure your relative is safe, then take the phone off the hook. You'll wake up refreshed far beyond your fifteen-minute nap.

- Cry once in a while if you feel like it. You don't always have to be strong.

- Count your blessings out loud today, maybe while you're driving somewhere.

- Change what you can about caregiving. Relinquish what you can't.

- Reach out to others. Consider having friends of yours or of your loved one over for dinner or to take a short outing. Your relative, if still alert, will enjoy the break in routine.

- Listen often to Christian or classical music. It will soothe and lift your spirit.

- Consider getting a pet. They live to please you, return your love a hundredfold, and never complain.

- When it comes to jobs, divide and conquer. In daily twenty-minute spurts, attack the closet that's driving you crazy. It will be straightened out before you know it.

- Court laughter like a teenager with his first crush.

- Look for the large place God sends you each day. "From my distress I called upon the Lord; the Lord answered me and set me in a large place" (Psalm 118:5). A place of distress is tight and oppressive, and we want out. But God can free us through a song, a sunset, a gentle word, a smile, or an unstructured hour.

Do You Know a Caregiver?

Caregivers are everywhere, and they're usually easy to spot. They are the ones who arrive late and leave early, who always look tired, and who either can't stop talking or say nothing at all. If one of your friends fits this description, you can help by avoiding certain things. Here are some caregiver no-nos your best friend wouldn't tell you.

- Think before you visit a caregiving friend. Maybe you're hungry for the chocolate mint cookies she used to bake. Perhaps you long for those cozy late night sharing times after everyone else went to bed. Hold it. For now, you need to put something else to bed—any thought of spending the night in your friend's home.

  If she's a caregiver, she's doing well to stay awake through dinner. Baking of any kind has become a distant memory. No matter how gracious your friend may sound, no matter how brief your upcoming visit, don't stay with her. She's simply not up to it. Stay in a motel or with other friends. But *never* stay with a caregiver.

- Park your children somewhere else if you visit a caregiving friend for an hour or less. It's not that she doesn't like your children. It's that she's worn out and has no energy—even for peanut butter sandwiches.

189

- Don't ask a caregiver to do one extra thing. No quick loads of laundry, no packing snacks to eat on the road. Beyond her enormous daily demands, anything is too much.

- No matter how awful she looks, don't say a thing. Her mirror still works.

- Avoid timeworn clichés: "Lean on Jesus." "Put it all in God's hands." "Keep your chin up." "This is God's will." "What a privilege it was to take care of my mom." She knows those things already and is doing all she can. Don't add to her guilt.

Would you still like to help—really help—your caregiving friends? Below are some suggestions any caregiver would welcome.

- When you see your friend, ask first how *she* is—*not* her relative. Everything in her life is revolving around somebody else. Ask about her. Give her time to answer, then listen while she does. You don't need to offer pearls of wisdom for everything she says—just a sympathetic ear.

- Use what's available in your life. Send an encouraging or funny postcard or note every month or so. Take cookies over once in a while, or fresh apples from your tree. Our neighbors were truly supportive. Gerda Glindeman, who specializes in wonderful homemade jam, delivered a jar to Penny every few months. And Jackey Eymer, sensitive to Penny's adjustment to the cold winters, sewed her a luxurious, long-sleeved flannel nightie, complete with easy Velcro closures on the cuffs. She also arrived regularly at special seasons, bearing a basket of candy at Easter, a ceramic pumpkin at Halloween, and chocolate hearts for Valentine Day.

- Set up a Dutch-treat breakfast or lunch together from time to time. Go to a restaurant, so the caregiver has a chance to be waited on. During your time together, ask how you can help. Respect your friend's schedule by limiting your time to an hour or so.

- Once in a while, call your friend and arrange a day for you to take dinner. Do the whole thing: main course, salad, rolls, and dessert. Put everything in foil pans so she won't have to bother returning clean dishes.

- Set up a time in advance when you will stay with your friend's relative, or take him out. This gives the caregiver precious hours of relief—and the fun of looking forward to it— and provides a most welcome change of pace for the relative.

- Remain positive. Avoid making negative statements to any caregiver, such as, "Why are you putting yourself through this?" Her reasons for home caregiving are complex and deeply personal. You'll help most by accepting her decision in a positive way.

- Announce your intention to perform a specific seasonal chore for your friend: mow her lawn, wash the storm windows, hose the patio, clean the house, shampoo the carpet in her relative's room, or take a load to the dump. Then be sure to do exactly what you promised.

- Remember the expenses involved with caregiving. Does your friend need financial help? If you can, assist with a loan or outright gift. Or organize a community or church fund-raiser.

- Help by doing the things you do well. Do you have a gift of organization? Do you possess

special professional skills? Should *you* start a
caregiving support group?

- Pray daily for the caregivers you know, and for
  others around the world. Remain sensitive to
  their special needs.

The Rewards of Caregiving

Caregiving is no picnic—that's why this book was
written. Yet the majority of people who provide home care
for a loved one are forever grateful they did so. Caring for
Penny was the most difficult thing we've ever done. In
looking back, however, we realize it was God's gift to us.
Such a perspective comes late in caregiving. Before that, it
must be taken on faith.

God refined and built my character as I cared for
Penny—sanding and polishing its many splintered and
gnarled places. Caregiving forced me to acknowledge how
Penny had hurt me. It made me admit my confusion,
bewilderment, frustration, and pain. Because Penny lived
with us, I couldn't simply walk away from it all.

Caring for her also provided opportunity for my healing, though that didn't happen overnight. It was up to me
to initiate help and be willing to accept it.

I had to come to a place where I was ready to acknowledge my own sin and receive Jesus' healing. Had Penny
lived somewhere else, I'm not sure that would have happened. Home caregiving slides every relationship under a
microscope.

It's pretty easy to talk about serving others. Caregiving
puts shoe leather to the intention. "Truly I say to you,"
Jesus told His disciples, "to the extent that you did it to
one of these brothers of Mine, even the least of them, you
did it to Me" (Matthew 25:40).

Penny was with us because she was one of the least.
Her thinking confused, her body beyond normal function
or repair, she depended on us for every need, large or
small. Did I skip to her room at the start of each day, joy-
ously eager to serve Christ by caring for her? Hardly.

But as months and years of caring for her passed, Jesus revealed Himself to me more and more. It was one thing to say that I was serving Jesus by taking care of Penny. It was quite another to learn to do it. As I realized the privilege that was mine, I could only drop to my knees before Him.

A few of the caregivers quoted in this book are finished with their caregiving seasons, but the majority are not. Most are home caregivers, though some provide across-town help. All were asked if they are now glad that they provided care. A sampling of their answers provides continual encouragement.

- "Yes, I am. She had a year of being warm, clean, and very well fed. And she had the opportunity to be part of our family" (David Sprowle).

- "Yes. It was a year of her life that we made easier for her. She helped us for many years with our children, and I feel we have somehow repaid her for all she did" (David's wife, Mary Lou Sprowle).

- "Yes, a thousand times yes! The experience is very hard, yet there is a richness it brings to life when God allows you to experience a caregiving situation. Our farm was Mom's home, and this is where she stayed" (Steve Kerns).

- "I believe we will be forever thankful. We live in a world which encourages us to go for self-fulfillment and self-interest. Caregiving cuts right at the heart of that . . . and allows us the privilege of slowing down to listen and keep pace with an older person" (Ted and Jane Hutchinson).

- "They were my parents and I am an only child. The most important help was my parents' love and appreciation for what we did for them" (Husband of an anonymous caregiving team).

- "It was an awesome privilege and we wouldn't have missed it for the world" (Kaye Kepple).

- "Curiously, while I personally do not wish to be a burden on any of my own children (does any man?), I am more inclined to believe in the sharing of ourselves with others. An old person in the home has a tremendous 'plus' value for grandchildren, who often acquire more values from her than from busy parents. A little child having difficulty learning to read, learns from Grandma learning to walk again. They also get a sense of security otherwise missing—if my parents love poor old Grandma, they'll love me if I'm hurt. The kids got *so much*, including acceptance of life's setbacks in a way never possible otherwise. I rank caring for my mother among the few worthwhile things of my life" (John Patrick Gillese).

Those answers came from people just like you. Not one said the job was easy, but most would do it again. All learned to cope with their limitations, to accept their loved one, to simplify their lives, and to live one day at a time. They learned that the way to love their relative was to take care of themselves. Each day, pledge yourself to do the same.

"Lord, I feel whole again . . . . What I'm doing has meaning, because of You."

"I long to transform your every task, My daughter. You have only to speak My name."

"Even in this, Lord?"

"Even in this."

THE CAREGIVER'S PLEDGE

(1) Today I will give myself time to adjust to the complex world of caregiving.

(2) Today I will gear down for the long haul, accepting the fact that caregiving has no quick fix.

(3) I understand that what I'm feeling today is normal: anger, discouragement, exhaustion, loneliness, guilt, frustration, inadequacy, grief, and much more.

(4) Because I love (Insert your relative's name), today I am going to do one thing just for me.

(5) Today I will try to locate a caregiver's support group in my area. Then I will give it a chance by making plans to attend at least one meeting.

(6) Today I will network, being honest about what I really need. I will pray for eyes to recognize and reach out to the person God sends to help me.

(7) Today I give myself permission to feel angry and trapped, to grieve for what once was, and to cry.

(8) In God's perfect time, I will yield to Him the pain I have lugged around all these years, and I will accept His healing.

(9) As I work today, I will whisper a prayer for caregivers everywhere.

Chapter Twelve
One Day at a Time

A single caregiving survival technique towers above all the rest: maintaining your relationship with Jesus. Make it your life's highest priority. Pour out your heart to Him in daily prayer. Listen each day for His answers, as you give Him time to work.

Be flexible in your times of Bible reading and prayer. Seek the Lord in new places, even unorthodox places, at different times of the day and night. Reach out; take His hand, feel its strength. He is there, longing to pour victory, energy, and joy into whatever your day brings. Moment by moment, expectantly receive what He has for you.

To help focus your day on God, this chapter contains thirty-one devotionals, one for every day of the month. Each highlights a specific caregiving need and can be used over and over. Read the devotion, then take time to pray each day's prayer. In your caregiving journal, record the insights God gives for your unique situation.

Day by day, God is supplying precisely what you need. He is with you in each caregiving task and phase. He is intimately concerned with your feelings, thoughts, and everything you do for your loved one. As you turn to Him, He will pour abundant patience and power into your caregiving ministry. He will send it to you in small faith packages, one day at a time.

Read Psalm 34

"The Lord is near to the brokenhearted, and saves those who are crushed in spirit" (Psalm 34:18).

One evening about a year after Penny came to live with us, she sat on our deck for two hours in her wheelchair. Finally she noticed Bob reading a magazine nearby, and looked over at him.

"Bob . . ." she questioned, staring hard in his direction. "Is that Bob over there?"

Later, after we helped her into bed, Bob's eyes were sad. "It just tears me apart," he said, shaking his head. "She was the woman who sat through double features with me, seeing movies about cowboys. I asked if we could see it over and she said yes. We sat through both of them again. And now she doesn't know who I am."

Few things agonize a caregiver more than not being recognized. Giving care is an act of love involving two people. When your relative doesn't know who you are, your caregiving becomes an act of faith, understood and seen by God alone.

But even in that lonely darkness, He is there. He feels your heartbreak, and restores your crushed spirit. Where there seems to be no light, Jesus becomes your daybreak.

PRAYER: Lord, You know how it feels to come with a purpose, and not be recognized. Bind up my breaking heart. Shine Your light into my darkened world. In Jesus' name. Amen.

Read I John 3:16-18

"Little children, let us not love with word or with tongue, but in deed and truth" (I John 3:18).

Do you ever feel as if your family's having a tug-of-war, and you're the one being pulled apart? Grandpa's color isn't good, and he refused breakfast. Prom night's three weeks away, and you promised your daughter the dress of her dreams. Your husband never complains, but how many consecutive nights can any man stand tuna surprise?

What you'd most like to do is stand in the living room and scream. Then you'd wave a wand and they would all disappear—just for a while. Then you'd walk out the door and do the one thing you really want to do: buy a pale pink rosebush and plant it in the front yard.

It's easy to say "I love you." The test comes in living it out. Love means praying for eyes to recognize a free hour to cut out the dress, and then praying for energy to do it. Love means visiting with Grandpa, all the while assessing his condition, and wisdom to know what to do about it. Love could mean asking someone else to cook dinner tonight. And love should mean saying good-bye to all of them on Saturday, and buying yourself a pale pink rosebush.

PRAYER: Lord, help me to love the ones You've given me, including myself. In Jesus' name. Amen.

Read Joel 2:25-27

"I will make up to you for the years that the swarming locust has eaten" (Joel 2:25).

"I long to get my own life organized," confided a four-year caregiver. "I feel as if it's been put on hold. When he needs something, I drop whatever I'm doing and help him. I want to do it and he's grateful, but I feel as if my own life is made of air."

Caregiving turns all the other parts of your life into empty honeycombs. You may find energy and time to fill up one or two cells. But the others grow dusty and out of date, poignant reminders of things you once enjoyed. Perhaps you think about a project in the morning and make plans to begin what's needed: plant the garden, sew the curtains, take the course in oil painting. But by evening you're too tired to talk, and even thinking of such an undertaking is too much. Most of the honeycomb chambers of your old life will remain incomplete and unfinished.

Be a wise caregiver. Keep those old loves dusted and at the ready, because God promises you a miracle. Your life will not forever be on hold. As He pledged to Israel long ago, God assures you today: He will make up the years you have lost.

PRAYER: Father, it's hard to believe You can restore it all. Help me to remember that You fed 5,000 people with two fish and five loaves of bread. In Jesus' name. Amen.

Read Luke 18:1-8

"He was telling them a parable to show that at all times they ought to pray and not to lose heart" (Luke 18:1).

"It's so good to see you," I exclaimed to a friend after church. "Tell me how Bill is." I wondered about his progress in a long battle with cancer.

"He's so much better," she said. "The doctors are very encouraged." Tears filled her eyes. "I don't have words to thank all of you who prayed."

As she walked to her car I watched the spring in her step, and I thanked God for answered prayer. Things hadn't looked good for Bill in many months, and he and his wife had been very discouraged. So had those of us praying for him. We continued in faith, not always understanding, but confident in God's reasons for delay.

Are there things in your caregiving journal you've been praying for, but no answer has yet come? Don't stop! In today's parable Jesus told His disciples a story to show them that they should *always* pray and not give up.

Like the widow who kept coming to the judge, never stop bringing your prayer needs to God. He will answer them all. Not early, not late, but exactly on time.

PRAYER: Father, thank You for answers that come quickly, and for those that don't. Help me to trust Your delays. In Jesus' name. Amen.

Read Matthew 16:21-26

"Whoever wishes to save his life shall lose it; but whoever loses his life for My sake shall find it" (Matthew 16:25).

After Penny came to live with us, I tried everything I knew to squeeze more hours into the day. I constantly felt pressured and frustrated, unable to break free. I rushed through everything, but never caught up.

One day as I read the Bible for strength, I came across today's verses from Matthew. They described perfectly what was happening to me. I was clinging desperately to my life, yet could almost see it disappearing. "Let go of your plans," Jesus seemed to tell me. "Accept what I've given you. In that relinquishment you will find your life."

I read and reread the words, and finally gave in. "All right, Lord," I whispered. "I accept it all. You've allowed Penny to be here. I'm turning my own plans over to You. Teach me what I'm supposed to learn from this. And please help me find my life again."

As I yielded to His will for me as a caregiver, God restored my life in a way I never dreamed possible. Rebuilding what I feared I'd lost began at the moment I released myself without reservation to Him.

PRAYER: Father, I feel as if I have no control over my life. But You do. I give it to You, right now. Make of my life what You will. In Jesus' name. Amen.

Read Psalm 46

"The Lord of hosts is with us; the God of Jacob is our stronghold" (Psalm 46:11).

Do you remember the last hike you took? Think back to that experience, to the trek that challenged your body until you wanted to quit. Maybe you were high in the mountains during the warm summer. Or perhaps it was October, when campfire smoke floated far below.

The trail wound ahead, narrow and steep. Your mouth was dry, your breath short, your legs cried out for oxygen. Still you pushed on, poised for the trail to level off, eager for the shock of the summit's ice blue sky.

That experience is a long-ago memory. Now you're on a different kind of hike: caregiving. Each day is like a step up that winding trail, and unless you push yourself all the way, you'll stop. You are dead tired, and today care little whether you make the summit or not.

God, who never becomes weary, understands. If you are to reach the top of your caregiving mountain, wait for Him. Hope in Him. Allow Him to fill you with His strength, day by day, hour by hour. Focus and dwell on Him alone. Don't look too far up the trail. Calling on His inexhaustible power, take one tiny step at a time.

PRAYER: Father, thank You. Help me to think less about finishing the hike and more about Your strength along the way. In Jesus' name. Amen.

Read Romans 8:18-27

"In the same way the Spirit also helps our weakness; for we do not know how to pray as we should, but the Spirit Himself intercedes for us with groanings too deep for words" (Romans 8:26).

"It's so hard when he's depressed," confided a wife caring for her blind husband. "It's like there's a heavy weight in the room. I can almost feel it."

Struggling with the effects of a small stroke in addition to his blindness, her husband's occasional depression wasn't hard to understand. She focused on staying cheerful during such times. She tried not to leave him alone too much, sat nearby to watch the news, took him for drives, or started one of his books on tape.

She enjoyed a vibrant prayer life, but admitted she found it hard to know how to pray when her husband was discouraged. What a great relief to discover from today's Scripture that we don't always have to pray eloquently, with perfect words. We don't need to explain each detail of every situation to God.

When we whisper our inadequacy to Him, the Holy Spirit meets us in our weakness. He Himself prays for us with feelings far beyond our words. When we cannot pray, the Spirit takes over for us.

PRAYER: Father, this situation is so difficult. With all my heart I thank You for understanding, and for the intercession of the Holy Spirit in my weakness today. In Jesus' name. Amen.

Read Galatians 6:2-10

"Bear one another's burdens, and thus fulfill the law of Christ" (Galatians 6:2).

What's going on next door, or up the road? Does a truck arrive each week, and the driver push what looks like an oxygen tank up the front walk? Do you occasionally glimpse a family member out in back, pale and feeble in a cocoon of blankets? Does your neighbor shop at night? Is he or she inside all day? Is the yard looking down-at-the-heels?

Then there's every reason to believe your neighbor has become a caregiver, and maybe it's time you baked some cookies. When they're cool, arrange them on a pretty paper plate and give your neighbor a call. Find out when it might be convenient for you to visit.

Before you go over, take a few minutes to pray. Ask the Lord to give you eyes to see how you can help with whatever's going on. After you arrive, look around while you listen to your friend. What could you do to make things easier? You can't do everything, but you can do something.

Today's Scripture doesn't mince words about bearing each other's burdens. Perhaps you're not a caregiver, but someone you know is. Ask the Lord how you can help. Then roll up your sleeves while you wait for His answer.

PRAYER: Father, forgive my blindness to the pain all around me. Thank You that the smallest kindness becomes great when done in Your name. Amen.

Read Matthew 5:43-48

"Love your enemies, and pray for those who persecute you" (Matthew 5:44).

Few caregivers enjoy a perfect relationship with their loved one, although many do experience a rewarding season of giving care.

But sadly, thousands of others struggle with the reality that they simply do not like the person they are caring for. They may have always felt this way, or found themselves pulling back as illness made their relative demanding, critical, and impossible to please. Whatever the cause, many caregivers feel chained to a person that they would never seek out for a friend.

Jesus had firsthand experience with such relationships. His solution was a revolutionary command for His followers: they were to love their enemies and pray for those who persecuted or misused them.

Are you caring for someone you don't much like? Maybe that's something you've never admitted, even to yourself. And you doubtless have excellent reasons for your feelings. In spite of that, begin today to obey Jesus' command: regularly pray for the person you're caring for. Then stand back, and watch what God can do.

PRAYER: Father, thank You for shining a searchlight into this hidden corner of my life. Encourage my relative today, Lord, and fill us both with Your love. In Jesus' name. Amen.

Read Psalm 91

"He will call upon Me, and I will answer him" (Psalm 91:15).

As Penny grew weaker and more confused, our energy reserves sank below sea level. "We are exhausted thinking she's passing away," I wrote in my caregiving journal, "then she doesn't, and the whole cycle repeats. It's like being under a cement roller that never moves off."

The weight grew heavier as death approached. We hovered close to two things: Penny and Scripture. Especially Psalm 91. I read it almost daily, soaking up its promises of God's faithfulness, security, and protection.

Mornings were especially hard, and I'd hide my head in the pillow, wondering how I could possibly get through another day. I wanted so much to think about something else—anything but disease and death. But that was impossible. Caring for a dying person in the home is like being in labor: you can't concentrate on anything else until it's over.

That's where verse 4 came in. In my mind I'd imagine myself hiding under God's wings instead of my pillow. I'd feel their softness and their gentle power drawing me to Him. And I'd remind myself that God is faithful. He would not give me more than I could bear. Holding tight to that truth, I could begin another day.

PRAYER: Father, thank You that my loved one can pass away at home. But oh, Lord, it's so hard. Hold me close today. Be my shield and defense. In Jesus' name. Amen.

Read Philippians 4:5-9

"Be anxious for nothing, but in everything by prayer and supplication with thanksgiving let your requests be made known to God" (Philippians 4:6).

Caregiving is punctuated with one anxiety after another. I can't attend Bible study because Mom may try to cook, and set fire to the house. We can't take a vacation anymore, because Sam's embarrassed about eating in public. Dad's speech is slurred today, and his eyes seem glazed. Is he having another stroke?

How's your own anxiety quotient? Are you borrowing trouble, forklifting tomorrow's problems into today? If so, notice the wording of today's Bible reading: we're to pray about everything *with thanksgiving*. That means having a spirit of gratitude about what God has already provided. Mom may set fire to the house, and Dad may have another stroke. But neither is true yet. God has given you a beautiful today, and He wants you to enjoy it with a thankful heart.

Make every need you have known to him. Pour out your anxieties to the Lord. But all the while remember His gift of this moment, and accept it with joy and thanksgiving. God supplies grace for each day in twenty-four hour doses.

PRAYER: Father, forgive my habit of worrying. Thank You for my home, clothes, food, and everything You have provided to meet my caregiving needs. Truly, I am grateful. In Jesus' name. Amen.

Read Matthew 11:25-30

"Come to Me, all who are weary and heavy-laden, and I will give you rest" (Matthew 11:28).

The nurse's aide and I eased Penny onto her left side, inspecting yet another skin breakdown. This one was only a quarter-inch across, and we discussed the best care for it.

Penny twisted her head around on the pillow, squinting up at us. "Will . . . will I be all right?" Her shaking voice was high and frightened.

"You'll be fine," we reassured her several times.

Too often during my season of caregiving, my thoughts centered on me: my fatigue, my isolation, my needs. I forgot that even in her confusion, even with her severe and advancing brain degeneration, Penny worried, too. Deep down, she knew she wasn't doing well.

That afternoon I smothered a toasted muffin in homemade strawberry jam. While Penny enjoyed it, I visited with her. That was always hard, because I had to do all the talking. She made one-word comments, smiling as I talked about the children, the weather, anything I could think of that might interest her. God used those tiny things to bring her joy and reassurance: a muffin, glistening red jam, spoken thoughts of the everyday.

PRAYER: Father, forgive me for thinking so much of myself. Thank You for showing me that I can lift my loved one's burden by sharing the smallest things. In Jesus' name. Amen.

Read James 1:1-6

"If any of you lacks wisdom, let him ask of God" (James 1:5).

"Did you check on Dad?"

"Yes . . . the pain's eased up, and he's finally sleeping."

"But it's dinnertime, and he hasn't eaten in days . . . ."

"I know, but don't you think he . . . ."

Taking care of another person can be like stringing a bead necklace. We just get comfortable with the shape and design of one decision when it's time to add another.

Every conclusion, like the string of beads, brings changes: what, why, and how. Every new set of plans or treatment impacts those already in place.

If ever we need wisdom, it is while caregiving. God's prescription is simple. He tells us to ask Him for the wisdom we lack. We're to come to Him in faith, not doubting, to receive His guidance in each situation. When we pray that way, we shouldn't be surprised when we experience an entirely new idea or a deep peace. That thought, that peace, is from God. We can trust what we feel and think, and move out in obedience to what He is saying.

PRAYER: Father, I'm scared. There are so many decisions, and I'm afraid I'll make the wrong one. Fill me with the wisdom I need, just for today. In Jesus' name. Amen.

Read Luke 2:15-20

"Mary treasured up all these things, pondering them in her heart" (Luke 2:19).

Did you ever think of Mary as a caregiver? She was, in the finest sense of the word. Mary understood little of what was happening to her, and had no idea of what it would all mean to her future. Yet she submitted to God's sovereign will, humbled by His clear call on her life.

When her little son, Jesus, was born, she moved quickly to care for Him—wrapping Him in cloths and placing Him in a crude manger close beside her. It wasn't long before shepherds arrived, eager for a glimpse of her baby.

Like caregivers everywhere, Mary stayed near to the One entrusted to her care. She kept Him warm, fed Him, and allowed others to visit. Today's Scripture describes yet another aspect of her care. As she watched all that took place, she pondered it in her heart.

You are also a ponderer, or you wouldn't be a caregiver. You see the end from the beginning, know much of your family's history, and sense the intertwined lives of you and your loved one. No, you certainly don't understand it all. But like Mary you faithfully give care, all the while pondering God's call on your life.

PRAYER: Father, sometimes I wish I didn't feel so deeply, but thank You for creating me as I am. May the meditations of my heart be pleasing in Your sight. In Jesus' name. Amen.

Read Matthew 20:20-28

*"Whoever wishes to become great among you shall be your
servant"* (Matthew 20:26).

Providing intimate care for a close relative is one of
caregiving's most difficult parts. For me, the hardest job of
all was emptying the Port-a-Potty. As I scrubbed it with
germicide, I thought of Jesus. Was this what He meant
about being a servant? Cleaning and disinfecting someone
else's commode didn't seem one bit spiritual.

But Jesus didn't say I had to be thrilled about what I
was doing. He simply told me to be a servant. Servants are
asked to do many things they'd probably just as soon skip.
The only thing that matters is that they obey, doing what
their master asks. Enthusiasm isn't a necessary part of a
servant's job description.

Some parts of caregiving aren't fun. They're downright
repugnant. But the most unpleasant task became easier
when I concentrated less on what I was doing and more
on serving Christ in the midst of it. Even cleaning the port-
able toilet wasn't so awful when I did it with a servant's
heart, for Him.

PRAYER: Thank You, Lord, for pressing me to the limit.
Help me to be a servant this one day, for You. In Jesus'
name. Amen.

Read I John 1:5-9

"If we confess our sins, He is faithful and righteous to forgive us our sins and to cleanse us from all unrighteousness" (I John 1:9).

"The chair is right behind you, Dad . . . go ahead and sit down."

"Give me some time, will you? Relax . . . you've got the rest of the day!"

But you don't have all day. You know that, but in his condition your father will never understand it. For the first time, like a rock skipped over a glassy lake, your thoughts skim over the possibility of pushing him into the chair. It's only eight inches behind him, yet he moves like a snail. Then your mind recoils, and you ease his trembling fingers onto the chair arms.

Perhaps you've played that scene, in one form or another, during your caregiving. Perhaps, in times of unbearable tension and fatigue, you have actually pushed him. Or worse. The memory is haunting, and you long for forgiveness.

It is right there for the asking, and today's reading tells how. Find a private place and confess all of your sin before God. Then set right any suffering you may have caused your loved one or others. Last of all, ask God to show you if it has all become too much, if perhaps you need help, if perhaps you should consider another arrangement. Ask, and He will answer.

PRAYER: Father, forgive me for the things I have done and for those I have left undone. For Jesus' sake, and in His name. Amen.

Read Hebrews 4:14-16

"We do not have a high priest who cannot sympathize with our weaknesses, but One who has been tempted in all things as we are, yet without sin" (Hebrews 4:15).

Did Jesus ever feel trapped? Did He ever think He was a failure? Suspended high on the cruel cross, He surely felt all that and far more.

From the beginning of His ministry He understood that by earthly standards, it would fail. He realized that He would be despised and rejected by men, and ultimately put to death. He knew the end from the beginning.

In your situation today, He understands. He has been there, and knows what you feel. But there is more. He walks with you as you carry tray after tray down the hall and back again. He stands near as you struggle with the necessity of finding a care facility for a loved one. He waits nearby as you push the fifth load of sheets into the washing machine. He wipes away your tears as you fail again and again to surrender past pain. He understands. Jesus identifies with every weakness you have. Wherever you go, He has been.

PRAYER: Father, such knowledge causes my heart to burst with praise! To think that You understand me so completely . . . it is too wonderful to bear. I can only whisper, "I love You, Lord." In Your name. Amen.

Read Luke 1:30-37

"Nothing will be impossible with God" (Luke 1:37).

What is your secret dream? Would you like to write a newsletter to encourage the handicapped? Become a maritime engineer? Learn to fly? Start a day care for toddlers?

Maybe by now you're laughing, because those dreams are so locked up they might as well be from the ice age. Oh, your dream used to seem possible. That idea, that goal you once had seemed attainable with planning, hard work, and persistence. But that was before you became a caregiver.

Now you're doing well to vacuum the house and talk Mom into taking a bath. She's doing pretty well, except for her mind, and it could go on like this for years. You expect little to change, other than your plummeting energy level.

"Nothing will be impossible with God." Absolutely nothing. He is toughening you through your present trial. He is fortifying you with strength today—strength you will need to fulfill your dream. He knows your heart and loves you with an everlasting love. Trust His timing. Tomorrow is closer than you can imagine. God is even now laying the foundation of your dream.

PRAYER: Father, help me to remember that dreams testify of my faith in You. Forgive me for letting today blind my vision of the tomorrow You have planned. In Jesus' name. Amen.

Read Ephesians 4:29-32

"Be kind to one another, tenderhearted, forgiving each other, just as God in Christ also has forgiven you" (Ephesians 4:32).

" 'Bye, Mom," called a caregiver's brother from the front door. Then he hurried back through the living room and knelt beside her wheelchair, folding his mother in a long hug. "I love you, Mom—see you next month!" A final wave, and he was gone.

My friend described that tender farewell a few days later. "It made me want to throw up," she admitted. "He swoops in here for eight hours once a month and does absolutely nothing except eat and fuss over Mom. After he leaves, it takes me three days to get her back to normal. I'm the one taking care of her, but you'd never know it!"

Her flushed face testified to deep hurt and anger. That situation was similar to thousands of other faithful caregivers. Everyone in the family, including her mother, pretty much took her for granted. Her brother refused to help, but it was he who received their mother's outpouring of love.

Today's reading confronts caregiving's anger. God asks us to forgive each other, even when our resentment seems completely justified. With Jesus as our example, we are called to sacrificial forgiveness.

PRAYER: Father, how often I nurture anger, reciting my long list of grievances. Help me to forgive as You forgave me. In Jesus' name. Amen.

Read I Corinthians 15:35-44

"So also is the resurrection of the dead. It is sown a perishable body, it is raised an imperishable body" (I Corinthians 15:42)

"Grandma!" She turned from the sink as Joshua's shoes squeaked on the linoleum. "That brown thing didn't die, Grandma! It lived . . . and it made a yellow flower!"

She pushed the dark hair from his forehead and knelt beside him. "Remember how that bulb looked last winter, Josh?"

"It was dead—all wrinkled and funny."

"And now what's happened?"

He took a deep breath. "It wasn't dead," he whispered. "It wasn't. Something happened under the snow. Come see it, Grandma!"

Watching someone we love go downhill is like planting bulbs in November. What used to be is now only a shadow. What will be seems only a dream.

By faith, we trust the shriveled bulb is not dead. By faith, we accept the promises of the Author of all life. By faith, we understand that death is only the beginning. The empty tomb patterns every springtime flower.

PRAYER: Father, may I never forget that You make all things new. Thank You that because of Jesus, there is no more death. In His name. Amen.

Read I Peter 1:3-9

"In this you greatly rejoice, even though now for a little while, if necessary, you have been distressed by various trials" (I Peter 1:6).

The rattling of frying pans jolted her awake. *He's wandered into the kitchen again*, she thought. *To search for something he's already forgotten.*

She heard the floor by the kitchen door squeak. "You going to sleep all day?" he shouted.

Weary, she glanced at the clock. Two in the morning. Hours before daybreak, but she would never get back to sleep.

Fatigue makes love a memory. If only he could still understand. If only he would smile, whisper "Thank you," sleep through the night. Worst of all is his complaining. His restless grumbling sears her being, makes her sometimes think of running away. She feels utterly alone.

"I am with You always," Jesus promised, "even until the end of the world." When she gropes her way into the too-bright kitchen, He walks with her. He puts His hands, in the form of hers, on her husband's shaking arm. In and through her tribulation, Jesus brings him reassurance and hope.

PRAYER: Father, thank You for the trial of my caregiving. Thank You for loving me enough to transform me into the person You want me to be. In Jesus' name. Amen.

Read Galatians 5:16-23

"The fruit of the Spirit is love, joy, peace, patience, kindness, good-ness, faithfulness, gentleness, self-control" (Galatians 5:22, 23).

When my season of caregiving first started, I tried to beat the clock. But jamming Penny's enormous needs into my already packed schedule didn't work very well. I was cross, hurried, and definitely not full of joy.

After several years, I learned I couldn't outrun care-giving's demands. The Lord taught me that the fruit of the Spirit doesn't ripen after all the jobs are done. The fruit grows in the midst of the work, probably because of it.

My tasks never ended. My days were never long enough. Interruptions washed over my life like waves on a beach. Slowly I learned to live with them, even to accept them. Strangely, love, joy, peace, and the other gifts of the Spirit matured in an atmosphere neither tranquil nor silent.

That discovery alone was worth the struggle. But I had to be in the crucible of caregiving to learn it. Drudgery, interruptions, and confusion come from the outside, most beyond my changing. The Spirit works from within, if only I give Him the chance.

PRAYER: Father, forgive my futile racing. Thank You for showing me that You work in any job site. Thank You for bringing gentleness and self-control in the middle of a ringing phone and sacks of groceries. In Jesus' name. Amen.

Read John 16:30-33

"In the world you have tribulation, but take courage; I have overcome the world" (John 16:33).

You probably began caregiving because you believed Jesus wanted you to. You weren't overjoyed about it, but the signposts of your faith pointed in that direction.

Weeks and months passed, and the novelty wore off. One thing after another changed. After you comfortably arranged the room, your relative needed a bulky mechanical lift. When you finally gathered strength to invite a few friends in for dinner, your loved one suffered another small stroke. Midnight vigils sapped your strength, and cozy dinners once again eluded you. The long-awaited nurse's aide, the one you took three weeks to screen, at last arrived. "Who are you?" your relative demanded. "Who let you in here? Who gave you permission?" And what you had hoped would be a halfway normal day disappeared like water down a drain.

Burdens and hardships are caregiving's warp and woof. From those tribulations God is weaving into your life new fibers of compassion, resilience, and strength. The caregiver's ongoing challenge is to focus less on the difficulties and more on Jesus. He commands us to take courage. He has risen victorious over anything we can ever experience.

PRAYER: Father, thank You for the tribulations that are so much a part of my days. Help me see the design You are weaving into my life. In Jesus' name. Amen.

Read Hebrews 11:1-10

"Faith is the assurance of things hoped for, the conviction of things not seen" (Hebrews 11:1).

Photograph albums fast-forward the past. As I turn its pages a tiny baby grows into a boy or girl, an adolescent into an adult. A bride and groom smile at the camera, fresh and young in wedding finery. Several pages later, maturity's patina deepens the love in their eyes.

Looking back helps me see what God has done in my family's life. And that look over my shoulder helps my caregiving. Just as the Lord numbered the days past, so He numbers the days present and beyond. He holds them all in the palm of His hand.

The photographs tell me that though time may appear to stand still, God is at work. Today may seem like forever, but it will pass like summer grass. The photographs build my faith in God's purposes. He had led me this far. He will lead me in the days to come.

PRAYER: Father, help me to grow in trust. Like yesterday's photographs, enrich my faith in Your silent workings. In Jesus' name. Amen.

Read Matthew 25:31-46

"Truly I say to you, to the extent that you did it to one of these brothers of Mine, even the least of them, you did it to Me" (Matthew 25:40).

One day I turned on Penny's television, placing the remote control on her recliner tray. She picked up her glasses in their case and pulled them halfway out. "This is the way to turn it off," she told me, pointing her glasses at the TV.

I patted Penny's shoulder, aching for her. That confusion illustrated her deterioration in a way no medical terminology ever could. Oddly, that episode also helped, jolting me to a deeper awareness of her total bewilderment.

Someone once said that the greatness of a society is measured in the care it gives its weakest members. That almost paraphrases what Jesus taught. But as today's Scripture shows, He went much further.

Acts of kindness do more than evaluate society. Jesus stated clearly that our tenderness and understanding are, in fact, done to Him. When I don't laugh at Penny, when I pat her shoulder, when I hand her a glass of water, I do it to Jesus. That simple knowledge revolutionizes caregiving. It becomes more than a job. Because I do it to Him, it becomes a ministry.

PRAYER: Father, today let me see more than my loved one's face. Give me eyes to see You also, Lord. In Jesus' name. Amen.

Read Isaiah 40:28-31

"Those who wait for the Lord will gain strength; they will mount up with wings like eagles, they will run and not get tired, and they will walk and not become weary" (Isaiah 40:31).

We'd had company all weekend, and through it all Penny's bed needed changing twice a day. Keeping up with the wash was out of the question.

Now it was Monday—a grey, damp spring day. Piles of sheets, pillowcases, and nightgowns greeted me. Too tired to face it, I shut the door, poured myself a cup of coffee, and curled up on the couch with my Bible. The most important part of this day wasn't scaling the mountain of wash. It was spending time with God.

The verses from Isaiah soothed my spirit and gave hope to my day. I spent a long time in prayer, committing each thing I needed to do to Him. The promise from the Isaiah passage renewed me from the inside out. As I waited upon God, He would give me new strength. I would move as if I were an eagle. I might even run through my day, yet not be weary.

Best of all, I could do the washing, cleaning, and care-giving, and not grow faint. The sky was still grey when I opened the laundry room door half an hour later, but I was smiling. God's promises were already coming true.

PRAYER: Father, thank You for renewing me exactly where I am. Forgive me for putting You last in my day. In Jesus' name. Amen.

Read Psalm 139

"Thou didst form my inward parts; Thou didst weave me in my mother's womb" (Psalm 139:13).

Caregiving lasts for a season. But unlike other spans of time, we don't know when it will end. We believe that one day it will be over, and sometimes we pray it will be soon. And for every caregiver, in the fullness of God's time the last day dawns. Sometimes there is certainty that death is near. Other times there is no warning.

But a week or two or three later, we are alone. And there is a void. We set our loved one's room to rights, clean it, air it, and dispose of the medical equipment. The vice-like schedules disappear, we cease worrying about special diets, we keep no midnight vigils. Once again life is sweet in its simplicity. Yet there is a void.

From the beginning God has formed us, and knows our hearts. He knows what we long for. He knows our desperate need for rest and healing. He understands that caregiving relentlessly drained us, yet paradoxically gave purpose to our days.

Now, perhaps, we are no longer so urgently needed. And there is a void. God will fill it to overflowing, exactly as He met every caregiving want we had. In the sweetness of His time, He will fill our emptiness.

PRAYER: Oh, Father, visit me today. Meet me in the midst of my hurting need. Fill my cup, Lord, with more of You. In Jesus' name. Amen.

Read Isaiah 49:8-13

"I will make all My mountains a road, and My highways will be raised up" (Isaiah 49:11).

"Why did this have to happen to us?" a grieving husband cried several years after his wife's death. Why did they have to pass through that dark valley of suffering? Why?

Most caregivers have asked that question. All of our activities center around helping our loved one, and many times we catch a glimpse of what God is doing in their lives. But we are too close to it, and often too tired, to see what He is also doing in ours. Only later, rested and with the perspective of time, do we begin to understand.

Our stretching, exhaustion, and anguished questions are not only for our relative. We cry out also for ourselves. God has worked powerfully in our family member's life. But He is working with equal might in our own.

As I cared for Penny I sometimes felt my hateful thoughts and anger were justified. But in calmer moments, I admitted that caregiving brought characteristics into focus that I didn't like in myself. God used that season in my life to refine me. I like the person I became through that trial. My mountains became a road. God's highways were raised up.

PRAYER: Father, thank You for loving me enough to sand the rough spots in my character. Help me to remember that sandpaper sometimes hurts. In Jesus' name. Amen.

Read Hebrews 12:12-15

"See to it . . . that no root of bitterness springing up causes trouble" (Hebrews 12:15).

"See you at the Christmas Eve service," I called to a caregiving friend.

"Are you kidding? Not this year you won't." She jerked her head towards her father's room, her voice tight. "It's like I'm a prisoner in my own home . . . ."

Fatigue, painful memories, and caregiving's never-ending demands often force open the window of bitterness. It slips in unseen, like damp night air through a crack. We don't realize it's there until we're shivering.

The sole antidote is daily vigilance. Over and over, we need to lock the window of our soul against a bitter spirit. Like bees in the garden, we must fly to the warmth and light of Christ's forgiving presence. Only He can evaporate the chill and remove our dark resentment.

But bitterness never disappears forever. It retreats to lick its wounds, still searching for unguarded windows. Sooner or later, on the cold winds of harsh words, a sharp tongue, or lingering guilt, it will creep in once more. We must daily be on guard, lest bitterness set up housekeeping in our souls.

PRAYER: I feel so weak, Father, and sometimes so far from You. Warm me, Lord, and keep me sweet. In Jesus' name. Amen.

Read Psalm 28:6-9

"The Lord is my strength and my shield; my heart trusts in Him, and I am helped" (Psalm 28:7).

"I don't know what's wrong with me," a caregiver sighed. "I give it to God, then take it all right back again."

A severe stroke had partially paralyzed her husband of forty years. Though his mind remained clear and he could live at home, his care and everything else landed squarely in her lap. Almost always cheerful, today her stress was plain to see.

"I think the problem is me," she added. "So often I forget to trust God and try to do it all myself. That always leaves me with a terrible dryness."

Today's reading assures this caregiver, and thousands like her, that God hears every prayer. His help surrounds her like a mighty fortress. During home care, it's not uncommon for a loved one to fall on the floor, or be unable to get out of a chair, even with assistance. Again and again God comes to the caregiver's aid. "I don't know where the strength came from," she'll say later. "But I got him up."

Just as He promised, God sent the strength. And later, when fatigue pulls the caregiver down, He promises to carry her like a shepherd carries his sheep. He is there. He is active. He is our constant help in every home-care situation.

PRAYER: Father, forgive me for trying to do it all myself. Thank You for your tender strength. In Jesus' name. Amen.

Read Matthew 28:16-20

"Lo, I am with you always, even to the end of the age"
(Matthew 28:20).

Every moment of the day, in every corner of the world, someone is taking care of somebody. In one way or another, they fear what you fear, hurt as you hurt, need what you need. Each day, some caregiving assignments end. Each day, others begin.

Through all of it Jesus is there, no more than a whisper away. No situation is beyond His control, no problem beyond His solving, no pain beyond His healing touch. He knows the number of hairs on our heads, the grains of sand on every beach. There is no agony He has not experienced.

From this moment on, pray every day for the caregivers you know and for those thousands you will never know. Pray they will open their hearts and lives to Christ, if they do not yet know Him. Pray they will allow Him to walk beside them on their caregiving roads. Pray their lives may be transformed through the reality of the living God. Pray they will know this day that He really is with them, as He is with you, even to the end of the age.

PRAYER: Father, I love You with all my heart. Thank You for walking beside me, even in this. In Jesus' name. Amen.

Part III

Appendix

The following organizations, books, magazines, groups, and agencies can provide a wealth of resources for your specific situation. Most materials are free or at low cost. To find out if a national organization has a toll-free number, call 800-555-1212. Also check your phone book to see if there is a local chapter in your area. When you can, reread Chapter 5, buy that caregiving notebook, and keep dialing!

Resources for Aging and Frail Elderly
Administration on Aging
Division of Technical Information and Dissemination
Department of Health and Human Services
330 Independence Avenue SW
Washington, DC 20201
(202) 245-0641
Write or call for information, services, organizations, and research on aging.

Aging Network Services, Inc.
4400 East-West Highway
Suite 907
Bethesda, MD 20814
(301) 657-4329
A national, for-profit network of private practice, geriatric social workers who help families split by distance. Write or call for description of program or fees.

American Association of Homes for the Aging
1129 20th Street NW
Washington, DC 20036-3489
(202) 296-5960
Provides information on community services, long-term care, and housing options for seniors.

Children of Aging Parents
2761 Trenton Road
Levittown, PA 19056
(215) 945-6900
Provides community education, sponsors national caregiver support groups, and offers comprehensive information and referrals for every state. Please enclose stamped, self-addressed business envelope and $1.00 to help defray printing costs.

National Association of Area Agencies on Aging
600 Maryland Avenue SW
Suite 208-W
Washington, DC 20024
(202) 484-7520
Provides specific referrals to all local Area Agencies on Aging.

National Assoc. of Private Geriatric Care Managers
1315 Talbott Tower
Dayton, OH 45402
(513) 222-2621
Write or call for individualized counseling, assessment, coordination of care (including long distance), and explanation of fees.

National Caucus of the Black Aged
1424 K Street NW
Suite 500
Washington, DC 20005
(202) 637-8400
Call or write for referrals, service, assistance, printed literature, and information on chapters and affiliates in 38 states. Designed to help older, low-income citizens, with special concern for the Black and other minority elderly.

National Council on the Aging
600 Maryland Avenue SW
West Wing 100
Washington, DC 20024
(800) 424-9046 or (202) 479-1200
Provides a complete list of excellent printed caregiver resources and current national caregiver support groups.

National Institute on the Aging
P. O. Box 8057
Gaithersburg, MD 20898-8057
(301) 495-3455
Write or call for pamphlets/information related to caregiving, including finances, nursing home selection, and research.

Resources for the Blind and Visually Impaired
American Bible Society
1865 Broadway
New York, NY 10023
(212) 408-1421
Call or write for catalog featuring large print or braille books and cassettes.

American Foundation for the Blind, Inc.
15 West 16th Street
New York, NY 10011
(800) 232-5463
Call for printed information and referral service.

Large Print Books
Thorndike Press
P. O. Box 159
Thorndike, ME 04986
(800) 223-6121
Write or call for complete catalog of large print books.

National Association for Visually Handicapped
22 West 21st Street
New York, NY 10010
(212) 889-3141
Call or write for information on large print loan library, visual aids, and other information about living with partial vision.

National Federation of the Blind
1800 Johnson Street
Baltimore, MD 21230
(301) 659-9314
Write for list of resources for the blind and partially sighted.

Resources for the Hearing Impaired
American Speech-Language-Hearing Association
Consumer Affairs Division
10801 Rockville Pike
Rockville, MD 20852
(800) 638-8255 or (301) 897-8682
Call or write for information and referrals for speech, language, and hearing disorders of all kinds.

Self Help for Hard of Hearing People, Inc.
7800 Wisconsin Avenue
Bethesda, MD 20814
(301) 657-2248
Write or call for details about the bimonthly journal, Shhh, *helpful resources and information, or referral to one of 240 national support groups.*

Books

A Grief Observed, by C. S. Lewis, Seabury Press, 1961

Caregiving—Helping an Aging Loved One, by Jo Horne, American Association of Retired Persons Publications (Scott, Foresman, and Company), 1985.

Caring for Elderly People: Understanding and Practical Help, by Susan Hooker, Routledge & Kegan Paul Ltd., London, 1976.

Emotionally Free, by Rita Bennett, Fleming H. Revell Company, 1982.

Family Health and Home Nursing, American National Red Cross, Doubleday & Co., 1979.

Home Care: An Alternative to the Nursing Home, by Florine DuFresne, The Brethren Press, 1983.

Parentcare—A Common Sense Guide for Adult Children, by Dr. Gary W. Small and Dr. Lissy F. Jarvik, Crown Publishers, 1988.

Taking Care—Supporting Older People and Their Families, by Nancy R. Hooyman and Wendy Lustbader, The Free Press (A Division of Macmillan), 1986.

The Help, Hope, and Cope Book for People with Aging Parents, by Patricia H. Rushford, Fleming H. Revell Company, 1985.

The 36-Hour Day, by Nancy L. Mace and Peter V. Rabins, M.D., The Johns Hopkins University Press, 1981. Warner Books, 1984.

The Loss of Self, by Donna Cohen and Carl Eisdorfer, W. W. Norton & Co., 1986.

The Practice of the Presence of God, by Brother Lawrence, Fleming H. Revell Company, 1958.

The Summer of the Great Grandmother, by Madeleine L'Engle, Winston Press, 1974.

Who Walk Alone: A Consideration of the Single Life, by Margaret Evening, InterVarsity Press, 1974.

Women Take Care: The Consequences of Caregiving in Today's Society, by Tish Sommers and Laurie Shields, Triad Publishing Company, 1987.

You and Your Aging Parent—The Modern Family's Guide to Emotional, Physical, and Financial Problems, by Barbara Silverstone and Helen Kandel Hyman, Pantheon Books, 1976 and 1982.

Resources for the Family
Family Service America
11700 West Lake Park Drive
Milwaukee, WI 53224
(414) 359-1040
Send stamped, self-addressed envelope, c/o Information Center, for a wealth of family-strengthening resources, help with long-distance caregiving, and referral to one of the 290 member agencies in the U.S. and Canada.

National Assoc. for Families Caring for Their Elders, Inc.
P. O. Box 3441
Silver Spring, MD 29091
(301) 593-1621
The major goal of NAFCE is to strengthen and support families in their caring roles. Write or call for referrals, encouragement, and workshop information.

Phone Book—*Check the first few white pages at the front for information and special services, including emergency first*

234

aid, community services, and phone communication resources for people with motion, vision, speech, and hearing disabilities.

General Resources
  American Association of Retired Persons (AARP)
  1909 K Street NW
  Washington, DC 20049
Provides caregivers with helpful booklets on various topics. For information, call Health Advocacy Services at (202) 728-4675.

  American Red Cross National Office
  17th and D Streets NW
  Washington, DC 20006
Contact your local Red Cross, found in the telephone directory white pages, for available resources, classes, and other services.

  Better Business Bureau—*Provides information pertaining to reputability of firms and organizations, handles complaints, checks advertising claims and selling practices. Check white pages of phone directory for BBB in your area.*

  Dental Care—*For referrals to reduced fee dental care and/or mobile dental units, contact your state or local dental society, found in the phone book yellow pages under Dentists' Referral and Information Service.*

  Emergency Call Systems—*Check with your local Area Agency on Aging, or call Life Line Emergency Response Systems: 800-642-0045.*

  Mills, Pollin & Associates, Inc.
  Home Health Care Management Consultants
  and Case Management Referrals
  1921 Augustus Court
  Walnut Creek, CA 94598
  (800) 728-4817
Assists clients and family to identify medical and social needs, develop a care plan, and provide advocacy.

National Hospice Organization
1901 North Moore Street, Suite 901
Arlington, VA 22209
(800) 658-8898
*Call the National Hospice Help Line, or write for information
and referral to a hospice program in your area.*

National Mental Health Assoc. Information Center
1021 Prince Street
Alexandria, VA 22314-2971
(703) 684-7722
*Write or call the Information Center for referral to national
support groups and other helpful organizations.*

Older Women's League
1730 11th Street NW, Suite 300
Washington, DC 20001
(202) 783-6686
Provides information on the concerns of mid-life and older women.

Public Library—*Your public library may have brochures
and other information about community programs for older
people. It may also offer large print editions of books, magazines,
tapes, and records. Also check bookstores and church libraries.*

The National Association for Home Care
519 C Street, NE
Stanton Park, Washington DC 20002
(202) 547-7424
*Write or call for information regarding monthly magazine,
Caring, plus free brochures on a multitude of caregiving subjects.*

The National Rehabilitation Information Center
8455 Colesville Road, Suite 935
Silver Spring, MD 20910
(800) 34N-ARIC or (301) 588-9284
*Contact for research, products, and resources related to the needs of
people caring for others with physical limitations, and for referrals.*

United Way—*Your local United Way organization, listed in the phone book's white pages, offers comprehensive referrals to appropriate resources in your area.*

Government Resources

County Extension Office—*Check the local government listings in your phone directory. County Extension Offices are located in each county of the United States, and may have brochures and other information about home health care and finances for older adults.*

Public Health Department—*Look in the phone book's white pages under city, county, or state government listings. May provide senior health screening, senior nutrition program, referrals, home care, transportation, immunizations including travel and flu shots, education, and more.*

Social Security Administration—*Provides information and referrals as needed on Social Security, Medicare, Medicaid, and Supplemental Security Income (SSI). Also offers help in completing applications for old age, survivors, disability, and medical insurance. Assists in obtaining proofs of age, death, marriage, and medical evidence for disability benefits. Beneficiaries can also receive assistance with address changes, locating lost or missing checks, and certification of income for rent subsidy housing. Call the national toll-free number: (800) 234-5772, or your local branch found in government listings in the phone book, or under Social Security Administration.*

Resources for Legal Help

American Bar Association
1800 M Street NW
Suite 200 South
Washington, DC 20036
(202) 331-2200
Offers list of free publications and information for legal assistance. Does not make referrals.

American Bar Association
Lawyer Referral and Information Service
750 North Lake Shore Drive
Chicago, IL 60611
(312) 988-5760
Provides assistance locating a lawyer.

National Senior Citizens Law Center
2025 M Street NW, Suite 400
Washington, DC 20036
(202) 887-5280
Offers referrals.

Magazines, Booklets, and Newsletters
Caring, a monthly magazine published by:
The National Association for Home Care
519 C Street NE
Stanton Park, Washington, DC 20002
(202) 547-7424

Parent Care, a bimonthly national newsletter published by:
The University of Kansas Gerontology Center
316 Strong Hall
The University of Kansas
Lawrence, KS 66045
(913) 864-4130
Provides information and resources for both professionals and family caregivers. $20.00 per year, or write for free sample copy.

Who Cares? a 72-page booklet published by:
Andrus Volunteers
The Andrus Gerontology Center
University of Southern California
University Park/MC 0191
Los Angeles, CA 90089-0191
(213) 743-5156
Filled with practical advice for home caregivers of older persons, the booklet costs $8.42 in California, $8.00 elsewhere.

Nursing Home Resources
American Health Care Association
1201 L Street NW
Washington, DC 20005
(202) 842-4444
Offers free brochure, "Thinking About a Nursing Home?"

Concerned Relatives of Nursing Home Patients
P. O. Box 18820
Cleveland Heights, OH 44118
(216) 321-0403
Provides phone and mail assistance with nursing home placement.

National Council of Senior Citizens
Nursing Home Information Service
925 15th Street NW
Washington, DC 20005
(202) 347-8800
Provides consumer information, help, and referrals for all types of long-term care facilities and services.

Office of State Long-Term Care Ombudsman—*Look in your state government listings in the phone book, or call your local Area Agency on Aging for the number in your area. Provides information, and handles complaints and concerns related to any area of nursing homes or board and care homes.*

Resources for Specific Diseases
Alzheimer's Disease and Related Disorders Assoc., Inc.
70 East Lake Street
Chicago, IL 60601
(800) 621-0379   In Illinois: (800) 572-6037
The Alzheimer's Association is the leading voluntary health organization fighting Alzheimer's Disease (AD), through research, advocacy, education, and patient and family services. The Association's 200 chapters and 1,500 support groups in communities around the country provide understanding, guidance, and practical advice for families affected by AD.

American Cancer Society National Offices
1599 Clifton Road NE
Atlanta, GA 30329
(800) ACS-2345
Provides information for all forms and treatment of cancer, including counseling, support, and referral to programs such as "Reach to Recovery" for breast cancer patients, "Can Support" for cancer patients and their families, the "I Can Cope" group to help people face the challenges of any cancer, and "Look Good, Feel Better," for cancer prevention.

American Diabetes Association
1660 Duke Street
Alexandria, VA 22314
(800) ADA-DISC
In Virginia and metro Washington, DC: (703) 549-1500
Write or call for education, information about summer camps in every state, support groups, and material on every aspect of diabetes.

American Heart Association National Center
7320 Greenville Avenue
Dallas, TX 75231
(214) 706-1179
Call or write your local AHA affiliate for information on reducing your risk of heart disease. Available brochures include information on cholesterol, blood pressure, stop smoking, diet, exercise, and more.

American Lung Association
1740 Broadway
New York, NY 10019
(212) 315-8700
Call your local American Lung Association for informational material related to lung health and disease.

American Parkinson's Disease Association
116 John Street
Suite 417
New York, NY 10038
(800) 223-2732
Write or call for free, detailed information on Parkinson's, and referral to information centers, chapters, and support groups.

Arthritis Foundation
P. O. Box 19000
Atlanta, GA 30236
(800) 283-7800
For information and referrals, contact your local chapter.

Candlelighters Childhood Cancer Foundation
1312 18th Street NW, Second Floor
Washington, DC 20036
(202) 659-5136

Council on Stroke, American Heart Association
7320 Greenville Avenue
Dallas, TX 75231
(214) 750-5300
Provides literature on stroke.

Muscular Dystrophy Association
810 7th Avenue
New York, NY 10019
(212) 586-0808
Call or write for patient and community services, and for individual help and referral.

National Kidney Foundation, Inc.
30 East 33rd Street
New York, NY 10016
(800) 622-9010
Write or call for affiliate office in your area, information, education, and community resources.

National Multiple Sclerosis Society
205 East 42nd Street
New York, NY 10017
(800) 624-8236
Contact for information on local chapters, referrals, education, counseling, advocacy, equipment assistance, support groups, etc.

National Stroke Association
300 East Hampden Avenue, Suite 240
Englewood, CO 80110
(303) 762-9922
Provides printed and phone information, referrals to nationwide stroke clubs, and research information.

Parkinson Support Groups of America
11376 Cherry Hill Road, Apartment 204
Beltsville, MD 20705
(301) 937-1545
Write or call for information, referral to support groups, and a free copy of brochure, "Parkinson Patient Profile."

The Cancer Information Service
(800) 4-CANCER
Call for detailed, state-of-the-art information designed to help make informed choices about prevention, early detection, screening, diagnosis, treatment, clinical trials, research, unproven methods, and rehabilitation. Caring, trained listeners also make appropriate referrals and offer a wide range of free pamphlets.

The National Easter Seal Society, Inc.
70 East Lake Street
Chicago, IL 60601
(800) 221-6827
(312) 726-6200
(312) 726-4258 (TDD)
Provides information and referrals to stroke clubs, speech, and physical therapy.

Resources for Veterans

Department of Veterans Affairs—*To find toll-free number of regional office for your area, look in phone book under state government departments, Veterans Affairs. Call for information about hospitalization, medical care loan guarantee, vocational rehabilitation, education, survivor benefits, burial, and compensation for service-connected disabilities requiring home care.*

Disabled American Veterans
807 Maine Avenue SW
Washington, DC 22110
(202) 554-3501

Veterans and their families may contact DAV regarding benefits and services.

Ninety
by Paul W. Brumbaugh

"Would someone help me,
Would someone help me, please?
Please!"

> "Hi, are you all right?
> What do you need?"

"Who is this? No . . .
No, I'm okay.
Where's my teeth?
Oh, I've lost my teeth!"

> "Here they are
> By your hand."

"Where is my cane?
Oh . . . I'm going crazy!"

> "Here's your cane
> On your chair."

"What time is it,
Is it bedtime?"

> "It's early. Besides
> It's your birthday,
> Your ninetieth birthday.
> There's cake and ice cream."

"Oh, that's nice, thank you . . .
Thank you . . . ?"

> "Trevor, your grandson . . .
> With the beard."

"I don't like beards."

"I wish I were nineteen, not ninety.
I had so much life, I was beautiful.
Bernie would drive down Selby Lane.
He would stop by the river.
We would walk hand in hand
And wade in the freezing water
And he would splash at me.
He would always splash me.
We would sit on the shore
And roll our toes in the sand.
He would put his arm around me
And try to kiss me.
He was so fresh!

"Nothing is fresh anymore.
I can barely see.
I can hardly walk.
I have nothing to do.
I wish I would die!"

"Oh, someone help me!
Someone help me, please . . .
Please!"

                              "Are you all right?"

"Bernie?"

                              "No, I'm Trevor
                              Your grandson.
                              What do you need?"

"Oh, nothing . . . maybe a cookie."

                              "There will be cake soon."

"Cake? What for?"

                              "Your birthday,
                              Your ninetieth birthday."

INDEX